NO SAFE HAVEN

ODYSSEUS sails - equipped for war

Cover picture showing devastation at Bari
by kind permission of the Imperial War Museum
(Negative Number A12745)

NO SAFE HAVEN

*told for the first time - an epic story of endurance by the
Allied Merchant Fleet in the Mediterranean - from the
Barbary Coast to Bari - 1942 to 1944*

George Glenton

NAVIGATOR BOOKS

Published by Navigator Books
Ringwood, Hampshire

ISBN 0 902830 44 9

Typeset by Moorhouse Typesetters
Printed by The Cromwell Press, Melksham, Wiltshire

Acknowledgement

I am extremely grateful to those individuals who so promptly and generously came to my assistance with further information on some of the many ships referred to in this book, and for their help in tracking down and producing many of the photographs used.

In particular I must express thanks to Mr. R. Kruis at the Netherlands State Institute For War Documentation Library in Amsterdam; to Mr. W.D.G. Korff, archivist at Nedlloyd Group's headquarters in Rotterdam; to Mr. Paul Kemp at the Photographic Library of the Imperial War Museum in London; to Mr. Cliff Parsons of the ever-helpful World Ship Society's Photo Library; to the staff of P&O Group's Public Relations Department, and the staff at FotoFlite, New Romney in Kent for their valuable co-operation.

Lastly, but by no means least, to my wife and former journalistic colleague Nancy who once within a decade of the events related accompanied me, as a passenger, in one of K.N.S.M.'s smallest steamers even older than the *ODYSSEUS*, and enjoyed every moment of its comfort and cuisine - an experience which in no way inhibited her much valued sub-editorial attention to the manuscript.

INTRODUCTION

In the autumn of 1942 the tide of war, which for so long had seemed on the ebb in Europe and North Africa, was about to change for the Allies. Under a cloak of secrecy, stringent even for war time, their combined land, sea and air forces were to surge forward in a flood of boldly planned operations which, within a year, would clear the enemy from Africa, re-establish control of the Mediterranean and carry the war into Southern Europe.

Such massively organised expeditions, on a scale then unprecedented, depended almost entirely for their success on the supply lines maintained by the ships and crews of the Allied merchant fleets carrying the men and equipment, munitions and fuel directly from Britain and America. In the forward supply zones they were to rely extensively on an armada of smaller merchantmen, peremptorily assembled and sent out from Britain to tranship much of those urgent essentials to the front line ports.

It was a fleet made up of ships designed essentially for peacetime trading and only hastily adapted for war, cargo carriers of many types, flying not only the red ensign, but also the flags of nations then under enemy domination whose crews, in voluntary exile, were bravely determined to contribute to the eventual freedom of their occupied homelands.

Though this books is mainly concerned with the adventures of only one of them, if it should be dedicated to anyone at all it must be to the crews of all of them, and especially to the memory of those who dauntlessly forfeited the ultimate joy of that longed-for reunion.

That my involvement came by chance, readily seized, was not always a matter for subsequent jubilation. There were times when I could have wished to be in some other ship on some other sea, yet never a time when I would have wished to be with another crew.

She was old and cramped, often hungry, and never an easy taskmaster, yet she had that endearing tendency to survival which alone engendered such loyalty as to hold me in her thrall. It was a feeling shared with others and that is why this story is mainly about her.

Most of the events chronicled, though still vivid in my mind, owe much of their detail to an ingrained habit for making notes, brought about when I was thwarted in my first ambition to make the sea a profession. Whole fleets of ships lay idle at that time and I was indentured to become a journalist instead.

When the chance came early in the war to catch up with the sea-time I had lost, the urge to qualify in that calling also before it ended, was too strong to resist. No nautical transformation could, by that time, eradicate the instinct for scribbling facts and the notes made then have proved invaluable in presenting this contemporaneous tale of the sea.

Should explanation be needed for its long delay I can only remind readers of the necessary censorship of that time which would have made its publication nearer the events a half-told story at best, a prospect which no journalist, and certainly no sailor, would have relished. I make no apology for burying those logbooks away, only for not coming across them again much sooner.

CHAPTER ONE

Only once, some months before, had I made what could truly be described in nautical terms as a pierhead jump, a last minute scramble over the rail of an outward bound ship with my gear landing beside me as she left the quay. It was not unusual in wartime.

Now happily, and more by a chance of the moon's phase than any administrative contrivance, there were to be no acrobatics. My response to a cryptic, eleventh hour summons had beaten the tide with just time enough to allow the briefest introduction to the shipmaster whose impatience so plainly proclaimed our urgent departure.

Captain Ruig was a Hollander and portly, in a uniform whose pre-war cut might well have dignified the bridge of some more impressive vessel than the one I was about to join. I could only think of Tasman and Van Tromp. Somehow he competently fitted such images and for me it is was enough. Yet it was the name of his command which most captured my imagination.

In some inspired moment in some halcyon period long before, her mercantile owners had chosen to call her *ODYSSEUS*, an eponym for me to conjure with.

To accept a berth in any ship unseen, destination unknown, remained a gamble, but at least her name held the tantalising suggestion of excitement beyond the realities of modern war. It was a notion even the unsmiling demeanour of her Captain could not entirely dispel.

He eyed me with no discernible enthusiasm, just a trace of relief perhaps that I had turned up when I did and was apparently competent to fill the gap in his crew list. He spoke English with a gruff fluency, but there was no time for any conversation beyond the most basic essentials.

When the hurried formalities were over he made sure I knew where *ODYSSEUS* lay, glanced warningly at his watch and strode from the agent's office. She was lying on the far side of the docks at Port Talbot and I soon caught up with him at the ferry landing where he was imperiously holding back the steam launch.

There were questions I might have asked him about the ship and her crew, but he remained aloof and volunteered no information, even when we were alone on the other side. When I asked him how long we might be away, his hard stare and noncommittal reply indicated clearly that our future was as much a mystery to him.

ODYSSEUS lay in calm isolation, in a far berth beyond an idle coal hoist. The immaculate Dutch flag at her stern was an immediate focal point. Against the leaden sky its red, white and blue panels proudly proclaimed the bright hope for a motherland temporarily in thrall.

She was down to her marks, perhaps a little over for so late in the year. Her derricks were stowed and clamped. Her decks and hatch covers had been freshly hosed of the grime which bunkering so liberally bequeaths and, from the crackle of steam at her windlass and the hiss of its impatient power elsewhere, she was in all respects ready for sea.

Looking down on her it was easy to acknowledge her ocean potential, but her peacetime role in the pattern of commercial voyaging remained a puzzle. She was old, launched, I guessed, about the time I was born and diminutive, with raised fo'c'sle, short poop and high midships section.

Her two disproportionately large lifeboats and the davits from which they hung were obvious wartime replacements which, with some ungainly additions to her accommodation amidships and bulky protection to her bridge and wheelhouse, gave her a somewhat top heavy dimension. But there was no doubt if an astonished Homer had been around with his Grecian galleys in mind *ODYSSEUS* would have aroused, in him, much greater emotion.

The urgency was to get aboard, but a keen compulsion to note her armament revealed three 20mm Oerlikon guns, two in nests on either wing of the lower bridge and one aft, with twin Marlin machine guns mounted on the boat deck abaft the funnel. In such cramped conditions, restricting most fields of fire, they nevertheless looked reasonably formidable.

By this time the Captain had disappeared aboard, but a cheerful hail from a wiry figure in a fisherman's jersey resolved the immediate problem of where to stow my gear. Joe Stoakes wore a battered felt hat jammed hard down over a ruddy face and reassuring grin. He was from Grimsby and welcomed me as a fellow countryman before loudly passing on the information to someone who was out of sight.

Then he grabbed my baggage and headed for the fo'c'sle leaving me to seek out the mate. I found him in a cabin on the starboard side marked "Erste Stuurman". He was short and rubicund and brass buttoned as befitted his authority, but not without an understanding glint to his eye. Simon de Jong was clearly a softer touch than the old man I sensed, but guarded about it.

He hoped I had not missed my lunch and sent me off to find some, if I could, in the remaining minutes we lay alongside. It was a kindly thought shattered, as I went forward, by the tinkle of the bridge and engine room telegraphs sounding the "stand-by". I had barely enough time to change into working gear before the activity on deck indicated we were about to get under way.

Seeing the fo'c'slehead was well manned I headed for the poop where the second mate was in charge. The tweede stuurman was tall, thin and pensive and was waving his unlit pipe to relay the orders.

They were being carried out with patient anticipation by a cloth capped Dutchman in control of the warping winch, and by a younger sailor who was coiling rope as the moorings came in. When the drumming stopped and we were moving towards the lock, the one in the cap introduced himself with a smile as Jacob van Ommeren. "Call me Jim", he said.

His companion shook hands, told me his name was Eric Adams and that he hailed from Erith on the Thames. The second mate had begun worrying about the fenders and Jim with a broad wink said: "Don't let him get his hands on them. He has lost too many already."

Whilst we were in the lock waiting for the water level to rise I learned from them, with some surprise, that the *ODYSSEUS* carried only six sailors, three Dutchmen and three Britons. For watchkeeping purposes it was unusually small if we were not to stand watch-and-watch, an arrangement which would never give us more than 4 hours below. It would be an exacting cycle on a deep sea voyage, particularly in wartime.

Jim, who saw my dismay, quickly assured me it would not work out quite like that. It was an Amsterdam practice he explained and was quick to tell me he came from Rotterdam. He promised to explain it later claiming it was too complex a custom to expound quickly to anyone whose experience was limited to ships sailing from any other port in the world.

As we headed towards Mumbles Roads, the second mate told us we would be anchoring there to await the compass adjusters. It was a routine procedure in which a ship is swung through the compass card whilst adjustments are made with magnets to her standard binnacle to correct, so far as possible, the effects of her residual magnetism.

Jim said: "I hope someone has told them what's in our holds - they'll need plenty of magnets." Seeing the blank look on my face he apologised and was surprised I hadn't been told. It was an important question in wartime and Jim and Eric Adams soon filled me in. It only deepened the mystery of our destination.

The *ODYSSEUS*, I learned, was a floating arsenal and high-octane fuel carrier. In number one hold, which ran aft from the collision bulkhead beneath the fo'c'sle, were stacked thousands of gallons of aviation spirit in small flimsy cans, each cushioned only from its neighbour by a cardboard outer cover.

In number two hold beyond that was a closely packed cargo of bombs, mortar ammunition, anti-tank mines and other military hardware. Number three hold, under the after deck beyond the boilers and engine room, was filled with artillery shells with a small consignment of composite rations to top up the load.

My first reaction was to understand the somewhat saturnine manner of the monosyllabic Captain Ruig. But my informants had not quite finished.

Somewhere among that lot, I gathered, was a specially constructed container of detonating devices marked "Highly Explosive", well buried for its protection in the centre. There was, too, a further enigma - a clue which at that stage did little to help as a pointer to our destination. Before the hatches had been closed, I was told, cargo slings and wooden trays for its contingent discharge had been stowed on top of the volatile assembly.

The alarming nature of our intriguing cargo did explain perhaps the smooth, swift nature of our departure, unimpeded as it was by irritating delays. Someone in the port we had just left was no doubt breathing easily again.

As no watches had been set, apart from 2 hour anchor watches which we would all take in turns, I went along to the second mate to sign some more forms which needed translation. In the privacy of his cabin-cum-office, like most ship's officers of his status, he was burdened with paper work. His pipe, from which he was virtually inseparable I was to learn, was glowing well and he was less reserved.

He told me something of the ship's background and that of the company to which she belonged whose initials - K.N.S.M. - featured prominently on the various forms he was completing. The Koninlijke Nederland Stoomboot Matschappi, or the Royal Netherlands Steamship Company as I knew it, was one of Amsterdam's longest established and most highly reputed shipping companies with a pre-war fleet of sixty or more passenger and cargo ships.

They were mainly all steamers apart from the firm's flagship, the liner *COLOMBIA*, which had been taken over by the Royal Dutch Navy and had fallen victim to a U-boat in the Indian Ocean only a few months before. Another of their passenger ships, the *SIMON BOLIVAR*, had been a much earlier casualty of the war, being sunk by mines off Harwich in November 1939 whilst still a neutral.

She had been outward bound for South America which, with the West Indies, was a regular run for many ships of their fleet. They also traded in the East Indies and many of the smaller cargo steamers, some even older than the *ODYSSEUS*, sailed regularly to the Baltic, the Mediterranean and Adriatic, and as far afield as the Black Sea. When Holland was invaded in May 1940 the *ODYSSEUS* was one of those ordered to make for a British port.

For two years she had been engaged in coastal voyages and across the Irish Sea, and had spent much time in port awaiting the day when she could play some more vital role in the Allied cause. It seemed that opportunity was at least on hand. There was one other fact about her which did not altogether surprise me for I had already noted certain features that gave a clue to her origins.

Once, long before, she had flown the German flag. She had been built in Hamburg in 1922 and, before being bought by her Dutch owners, she had been named the *RUDOLF*.

Later in the engine room, where for their own canny reasons her Dutch owners had not seen fit to exchange perfectly serviceable fittings, I discovered that the dial on the highly polished answering telegraph still bore its original teutonic wording. She must have been one of the few ships in Allied service where watchkeepers were in the habit of responding to the imperative "Achtung".

The third mate, or derde stuurman, was looking for me to issue such items of equipment as the Ministry of War Transport deemed necessary for minimal protection or contingency. He handed me a steel helmet, a whistle on a lanyard and a lifejacket light and threw in a useful sheath knife with a keen blade.

He was young, red-haired and genial and not a company's man I gathered. He had been in the pilot service when Holland was invaded and had made his own way across the North Sea with little time to spare.

By far the largest and most powerful man aboard was the bo'sun or bootsman. He had a grin to match his stature and an imperturbable air. Any rare displeasure he reserved for what he saw as occasional unnecessary directions from above. Having already observed him from a distance it was clear he invariably knew what needed to be done and how best it should be carried out.

It was a surprise when he relieved me on anchor watch at six o'clock the following morning. Bo'suns, in all the ocean going ships I knew, kept no watches at all and enjoyed their full night's sleep.

There was no point in turning in again at that hour and he seemed happy to talk. He explained the mystery of how a ship with so small a deck crew could maintain a properly manned rotation of watches without depriving them of much needed sleep.

The *ODYSSEUS* did not follow the customary pattern of four hour watches. By an ingenious arrangement it had only two watches of that duration - the middle watch from midnight to 4.00am and the morning watch from then until 8.00am. What would have been the forenoon watch continued until 1.00pm. The afternoon watch of 6½ hours until 7.30pm was followed by a 4½ hour trick until midnight.

To change the daily sequence everyone got an extra watch below after doing three watches. This was made possible because the Bo'sun took his turn as seventh man. He was philosophical and told me it was not too bad in practice and in some ways had its advantages for the crew. I was happy to believe that wherever we were bound it was unlikely to be a voyage of long duration.

Breakfast in the fo'c'sle, which also served as our mess, was a culinary shock. It was different if not altogether indigestible. There was a large dish of something that looked like thin porridge, but turned out to be boiled barley, so unpalatable as to be spurned by all. Suddenly I missed that traditional sailors' standby, the much lampooned burgoo - a nourishing concoction of oatmeal cooked with butter and seasoned with salt.

Generations of sailors had thrived on it, often complainingly yet grateful for its sustaining warmth, particularly in heavy weather when the galley sometimes became the most dangerous place in the ship. Even in its lumpiest form, matched against the incongruent mass before us, it would have passed as haute cuisine.

The main course was a basin filled with herrings, marinated in the cask. At that early hour my stomach registered some protest, but conscious of several pairs of eyes watching for my reaction, I tried one and found it tasted good. Eric Adams, I noticed, was starting his day on bread and jam.

There was a large teapot which he and Stoakes warned me against because its contents had been so stewed as to make it undrinkable. But there was a coffee mill bolted to a bulkhead with evidence of freshly ground beans and a steaming coffee pot whose fragrance was more than agreeable.

My enjoyment of the herrings brought a word of benign approval from the older of the two Dutchmen who completed our deck crew. Jacob Ouwehand was from Katwijk in South Holland. He was short with tousled hair and marline-spike fingers.

He had been the skipper of his own fishing boat at one time and, learning that I came from Scarborough on Yorkshire's north-east coast, embarked on a joyful account of the many times he had been there in the herring season.

They were occasions I knew well, a memory I could share with pleasure of late summer days when the South bay was a mass of tanned sails, when the quays and crowded streets echoed the clack of wooden shoes. It was a nostalgic bridge which was to become a close bond.

The sixth member of the fo'c'sle, Jacob Harteveld, was younger and very blond. He spoke excellent English and was immediately helpful in introducing me to some of the more important translations of operational orders. In an emergency on watch I could see it might be of urgent necessity.

He was married to an English girl with a home in Essex and impatient to introduce her one day to his homeland. He was a keen seaman eager to get on and it was easy to see him wearing a stuurman's uniform one day.

There was a lot to be done on deck before *ODYSSEUS* faced the Atlantic. It was the time of the year when storms could be expected and everything had to be properly secured and all gear checked. Whilst swinging out the lifeboats one of the ropes intended to hold the starboard boat tight against its griping spar had carried away as we heaved on it depositing us heavily on the deck.

It was new rope and its deceptive quality gave cause for alarm. Someone might easily have gone over the after edge of the boat deck if we had pulled in that direction. There was a winch directly below and for him the voyage would have been over.

Our departure came soon and sea watches were set as the anchor cables came in. As I guessed, we were heading for a convoy assembly port and Milford Haven was an obvious destination. With November on us the sea was surprisingly light and the sun was warm and, by the luck of the rota, the trip towards St Anne's Head beyond Carmarthen Bay brought me a spell at the helm with a chance to sample her whims.

Under such conditions, heavily laden as she was, she behaved impressively, but I was left with the suspicion that in strong winds and heavy seas she would not be so easy to control. The layout of the wheelhouse was far from ideal. It had all the atmosphere of a protective bunker with no outside visibility beyond the small horizon the helmsman could glimpse through a narrow slit in the reinforced bridge frontage many feet away.

From his grating, positioned well back, the man at the wheel had no outward vision to the sides and it needed no prophet to foretell the degree of eyestrain soon to be inflicted by the faintest of binnacle lights. The compass card needed little translation with only the East and South cardinals seeming alphabetically strange, representing respectively Oost and Zuid.

By the time we entered Milford Haven I had come to the conclusion that, on the credit side, she was an encouragingly buoyant ocean vessel with a useful reserve of speed beyond her twelve knots.

The pilot directed us to a remote buoy where lay another small steamer, the *PENSHURST*, of which we were to see much more in the coming months. She was flying a red burgee, the B flag of the international signal code which at once indicated the similar nature of her cargo. Wherever we were bound it was certain she would be coming with us.

Unshackling one of our anchors in order to use its cable as a buoy mooring was an unexpected chore, and an indication that we would not be setting out on that adventure without some further delay. When I took the watch book along to the mate I found that the Captain wanted to see me.

His instructions were brief. I was to keep my ears open for aircraft and to take what bearings I could if I suspected that mines were being dropped. Returning the watch book the mate emphasised the orders with all the severity of a hopeful mentor, using a forefinger to pull at one of the pouches under his eyes and saying: "You keep a good lookout - eh? Een guid outkijke!"

I felt it safe to assure him that with the cargo we had, none of the crew were likely to be less than fully alert.

Having the first watch in the early evening gave me a chance to meet some of the gunners with whom the ship seemed abundantly endowed. There were four members of the army's Maritime Regiment and three naval ratings, who shared a specially constructed box-like compartment on the starboard side of the boat deck.

In charge of them was a Sergeant of the Royal Marines who shared a cabin with the assistant steward.

Sergeant Bunce was a veteran of the First World War who had come out of retirement, giving up a cosy shore job, to return to sea. He was perhaps the only man aboard impatient to get into action. In the meantime it seemed he nursed his wrath with a mixture of long suffering tolerance and that brand of criticism to be expected from someone used to much larger ships.

He was not too happy about his accommodation or the food and it seemed his malaria was troubling him, but on the whole it was comforting to have him aboard if only for his stimulating approach to our daily fortune.

It turned out to be a quiet night. Indeed the two days we waited for the convoy to move were, in more than one sense, the calm before the storm. The absence of any transient enemy activity was perhaps a more importance bonus than we realised.

The time was not wasted. Launches came and went between the ship and the shore, delivering messages and workmen, including a gang sent aboard to construct a hinged rail on either wing of the bridge to heighten the protection from the weather. I found the foreman measuring the drop between the bridge and the main deck to confirm their qualification for a danger bonus.

Because it was a weekend he told me they were already on an overtime allowance. He had noticed our red burgee and was also going to investigate the possibilities of a further danger payment. He claimed he had been at sea at one time and wished he could return to it, which I took with a pinch of salt.

We visited aboard the *PENSHURST* mainly to find out if they knew anything more than we did about the pending convoy, but found them as much in the dark. We came back with a supply of pickled onions of which they had plenty and Jim absentmindedly ate the entire contents of one jar, crunching his way through them whilst continuing a conversation in Dutch.

11

He looked sheepish when he found he had emptied it and said apologetically: "They are good for scurvy." It pleased him that we were amused. He had the widest seafaring experience of us all and behind his amiable smile was a wisdom acquired in ships of diverse nationalities, including British.

Born and brought up in Rotterdam he demonstrated a feigned tolerance for what he considered to be Amsterdam practices. If the *ODYSSEUS* had carried a carpenter, that would have been his rating, sharing quarters with the Bo'sun.

He had joined her for a break to steady his nerves, after being torpedoed I think, and on the coast she had suited him admirably, particularly when she was in London. He had developed a fascination for Madame Tussauds and for the speakers at Hyde Park on a Sunday.

His party piece was to imitate one whose antics he had particularly enjoyed. It was a comic turn he was persuaded to do for my entertainment and it was loudly applauded. Even the smaller Jacob, who maintained an on-going contention with Jim over his pipe smoking in the fo'c'sle, joined in.

Jim was a morale booster, as much for himself I suspected as for the others. He had a lugubrious side. He had been at sea when Rotterdam was so heavily bombed before the invasion of May 1940 and he had received no word of his family since then. It was a carefully guarded concern, but not difficult to detect in him, or in those others who had come to look upon the *ODYSSEUS* as a wartime home.

News aboard derived mainly from fragments of conversation picked up by avid ears or from elaborate conjecture following any sign of unusual activity in the distance. Speculation about our sailing time was rife, but no word came from the bridge. In Milford Haven one breathed only the strong air of the Atlantic, last letters had been written and we were anxious to get away. Rumour had it that we would sail in the morning.

CHAPTER TWO

For once rumour proved to be right. The concealed hand which controlled the discreet movement of such argosies was only evident to the trained eye. For a brief period there was an added urgency to the coming and going of fast launches whose spray sparkled in the morning sunlight. It alerted us to the fact that the deep was calling and soon there was no doubt.

There came the order from the bridge to unshackle our cable and to undertake the laborious task of reuniting it with its heavy anchor. It took us some time and the *PENSHURST* got away first, but we were not far behind. As we headed in file for the open sea with each ship flying its appropriate column and position flags it was plain to see that we were to form part of a considerable force.

Some ships I recognised from a previous convoy which had assembled in that convenient departure area, but then there had been no mystery about our ultimate purpose or destination.

All the ships manoeuvring that morning to find their allotted places in the formation were of similar size, most of them under 2,000 gross tons, yet they made a strangely assorted collection even for wartime. Mainly they were small cargo steamers of the tramp ship variety, but among them were several identifiable coasters almost certainly leaving their home waters for the first time.

The weather was mild with only a moderate sea and it felt good to be heading somewhere at last. After helping the Bo'sun secure the anchor cables in the spurlingates, the vertical pipes leading from the chain locker below the fo'c'sle accommodation, he reminded me it was my watch below.

The midday meal was a distinct improvement with braised steak and fresh vegetables. But for the knowledge that, at some time in the next ten days or so, any remaining contents of the ship's icebox would certainly be condemned, it might have seemed that the cook had made a special effort to mark our freedom from the shore.

The convoy was on a westerly course with the whole breadth of the Atlantic before us when I went on watch with Jim and the older Jacob, who was usually called Jaapy, that evening. The visibility had decreased considerably and each line of ships was striving to maintain some semblance of a straight file by showing their faint, blue stern lights.

Handicapped by his short stature the mate was suffering considerable frustration because of the height of the new weather dodgers. It was just possible from the helmsman's grating to hold in view the light of the ship ahead as we strove to keep a safe distance from her without dropping too far astern.

When that happened or if her stern swung widely or our head fell away even slightly, the blue light disappeared from the small aperture which was the helmsman's only field of vision.

Such conditions required the alert anticipation of the man at the wheel and imposed frequent alterations in revolutions, passed by the mate to the engineer on watch through the voice pipe. All the while the heavily laden *ODYSSEUS* made it clear she did not take kindly to such constant restrictions on her forward progress. She reacted boorishly to such checks and, with the weather on her port bow, responded occasionally with maddening slowness.

The mate tried holding her on a set course, but when that involved even more alterations it was a relief to be told to resume my hopeful pursuit of the blue will-o'-the-wisp. Jim knew what to expect when he relieved me at the wheel. Philosophical as always, he told me it would be different once the convoy increased speed.

Our slow progress continued all the next day. It had little to do with the weather which had not worsened appreciably. Either we were marking time it seemed or had with us some ships whose low maximum speed was holding us back.

We were still heading west and, for the following two days, continued to steer for those middle waters of the Atlantic where discovery by U-boat or by wide-ranging Kondor aircraft would give them no real clue to our eventual goal.

So far there had been no evidence of either; no depth charge detonations following suspect echoes from below and no sinister throb from any four-engined menace above the overcast.

Already I had reached the conclusion, mainly because of our restricted bunker capacity, that our first port of call might well be Gibraltar. Certainly many of the ships in the convoy would need their oil or coal fuel topped up by that stage.

From Britain it was a vital sea route used mainly by convoys carrying iron ore from Spanish and North African ports and was much contested by U-boats working in conjunction with the deadly Kondors operating from the French coast. They had attacked with devastating success.

At one stage, before the unacceptable losses caused all sailings to be temporarily suspended, the Royal Navy introduced its first escort carrier to the run. She was converted from a captured German merchant ship and renamed *AUDACITY*. On her first operational trip her fighters had accounted for one Kondor and forced at least one U-boat to dive below periscope depth.

That convoy had lost five ships to U-boat torpedoes and also the rescue ship *WALMER CASTLE*, to the bombs of another Kondor. I was reminded of it when I recognised in our present ranks, a year later, at least one of the survivors from that outward voyage. I remembered too that on that return trip without the carrier's support, the losses had been even more dramatic and included the loss of the renowned Tribal Class destroyer *COSSACK*.

It was a gloomy moment to recall that *AUDACITY* had only survived in those waters for about twelve weeks before a U-boat claimed her.

Eric Adams had also been that way before, I think, but we did not talk about it, perhaps because the weather showed signs of deteriorating and becoming much more of a hazard in close company. It was undoubtedly affecting some of those aboard, particularly the young lad whose main job was to keep the fo'c'sle in shipshape order.

After a brave attempt to overcome his seasickness he had taken to his bunk and left his sympathizers to do their own domestic chores. One of the gunners, a DEMS rating with red hair, won general admiration through his determination to stay on watch. It was his first trip and his stomach had rebelled from the moment we sailed.

How he withstood the fairground antics of the gun box on the poop was an object lesson in fortitude. Wherever we were bound Ginger was one man who could not wait to get there, if only to eat again without the certainty of almost immediate regurgitation.

His one concession was to swap positions with one of the army gunners named Ted Maloney, a Londoner of dry cockney wit, who seemed to positively enjoy the ups and downs of life in the after gun position. On the whole it seemed that the soldiers were less affected by the buoyant motion than their naval counterparts.

Sergeant Bunce who spent much time on the lee wing of the bridge appeared to treat the weather with some condescension, obviously looking upon it as a possible ally against premature attack.

Gun watches had been set from the moment of our departure and though we had no armament with sufficient range to worry any high flying Kondor, the low cloud base whilst concealing our presence provided such aircraft with excellent cover for low level attack.

Before I joined the ship the deck crew had nearly all taken short courses in handling particular machine guns and I already had that qualification. It was no surprise to learn that a rota had been drawn up for us to do an additional watch in the gun box where the twin-Marlin was mounted. As an acknowledgement of our supposed proficiency it was not entirely unwelcome.

It was an American weapon of remarkable simplicity with few of the many sources of stoppage with which the First War Lewis guns, issued to so many merchant ships, were cursed. So long as the belts which fed it were properly loaded it functioned as efficiently as a pneumatic hammer.

Its only failing was its restricted range and insignificant calibre yet, with every third round a tracer bullet, it was nevertheless a comforting supplement to our firepower and a hopeful front of discouragement against close attack.

Standing watch over it had other benefits I discovered. Its nest was positioned on the boat deck between the funnel and the radio shack whose sole occupant turned out to be a free spirit with a refreshing range of well informed conversation.

Jack Ridler was from Gloucester and was making his first trip as a radio officer. In order to maintain a twenty-four hour watch most deep sea ships carried three operators in wartime. Having only recently acquired his certificate he had been thrust in at the deep end as Marconi's only representative.

In peacetime members of such a fraternity could, and did, seek urgent advice from each other through their own medium, but not in wartime. Jack was very much on his own should problems arise, but having found his feet he seemed cheerfully unawed by the considerable responsibility emergency had imposed.

I quickly discovered he had an inquiring mind and an aptitude for intelligent debate. His interest in the work of the ship and in other people's problems was to make him a useful independent ambassador for the crew in general, particularly when matters concerning their welfare arose.

Personal radio receivers were strictly forbidden during wartime voyages, but there was a relay system with a speaker on a bulkhead in the alleyway separating the sailor's and the firemen's quarters. At regular intervals when circumstances permitted we got brief news bulletins and it was in that way we got our first intimation of our objective.

The consensus of opinion was that we were bound for West Africa to take part in a second attempt to establish a base at Vichy controlled Dakar. Other opinions, slightly nearer the mark, considered our destination would be Casablanca. But the news was of the Allies' successful landings at Algiers and Oran on the Mediterranean coast.

Following the Eighth Army's great success at El Alamein and the immediate advance through Libya, which had been the big news before we sailed, the purpose of our departure should have been obvious. Apparently the enemy had not guessed it either, but now it would be clear to them that our convoy, and almost certainly others, would be at sea.

The Vichy forces at Casablanca were, I think, still holding out and some members of the crew still believed it might yet be our objective. Others spoke more grimly of bases far to the east of Algiers which might, at some stage, be involved in the scale of the operation. It momentarily concentrated the mind on the heavy presence of enemy air forces in nearby Sardinia and Sicily.

For the time being we had other problems for that more enduring enemy, the sea, was showing her seasonal spite. When we had eventually altered course to the south we began fighting our way into a head sea with gale force prospects. Steering became hard work as the convoy struggled to keep its formation and to sustain those vessels less able to hold their positions.

One in particular, a small vehicle ferry with a high bridge, must have been giving her crew an awful time. She was obviously of very shallow draught and her wild movements suggested at times that she was about to do a back somersault until her broad, saucer-like bow crashed down again in a tempest of foam.

What she was doing in our company was anyone's guess. One could only hope that any urgent reason for her inclusion was sufficiently important to condone such torment. Other ships were making heavy weather of it and even *ODYSSEUS*, which had been shaking off the steep seas, began to bury her bows.

A discreet examination of the chart in the dim light of the curtained recess at the rear of the wheelhouse showed us to be somewhere in the latitude of Finisterre. By that time she had become very wet. Crossing the foredeck without getting soaked required dexterity and good timing.

The poor fo'c'sle lad was still in his bunk and collecting our meals from the galley was no guarantee that they would be delivered intact to the table. I noted that Joe Stokes, with his hat jammed hard down, had the trawlerman's knack of ducking under the bulwarks when a sea came over and escaping the worst of it.

The watches passed, but oilskins no longer had a chance to dry as their owners slept and the engine room became festooned with damp clothing. It was a misery on lookout and a pleasant relief to take over the wheel and join battle with elements which attacked us with such glee.

Their heaviest assault came on Friday - the thirteenth day of the month. It was the long trick of the day, the 7½ hours watch, and I was doing my second and final spell at the wheel when I heard a loud, sharp crack from somewhere on the boat deck, on the starboard side.

There was a lot of shouting, muffled or snatched away by the wind. Captain Ruig's head appeared from that side and he ordered the wheel hard over to port. By that time the commotion had increased. Minutes before there had been several men at close hand - gunners, the mate on watch and a lookout. Any one of them would have let me know what was happening.

Suddenly it seemed they had urgent work on their hands and I was left in the dark, fearing some serious catastrophe. The Captain returned to ring down for half speed and was quickly gone. When he came back he seemed much calmer and this time moved the telegraph to Stop.

From the sounds outside I concluded that a lifeboat had come adrift and remembered the dodgy rope we had previously replaced. But I had my own problems by then for without any way on her the ship's bows were falling off before the weather. Quickly the Captain was back to ring for some forward power to help me get her head into the wind again.

It was Eric who told me what had happened, a few minutes later. He looked as if he had been in battle. The guy on the forward davit had carried away and the boat had run wild for a while threatening to burst the bellybands and carry away its other lashings. The Bo'sun had saved the day by rapidly taking control, but at one stage Joe and Eric had very nearly gone over the side in the fight to save it.

Jim told me later that an unexpected roll had saved them and I guessed it must have been when the ship swung into the trough. Looking at the job they had done I could see that the boat was not going to get away very easily again with so many extra lashings, even if we needed to launch her in an emergency.

The four-to-eight watch, the next morning, was a stiff test of endurance. It was sleeting with such force that, on lookout, it was virtually impossible to face into the weather. We had dropped behind the convoy a good way to attend to our problem and though we knew the ships ahead would be displaying their stern lights it was considered safer for once to hold back until full daylight, if it ever came.

We were coming up on the convoy fairly quickly for *ODYSSEUS* had a good reserve of speed, but we expected to find other stragglers behind them and apart from the helmsman everyone on watch, including the gunners, was searching the sea ahead. All had become wet to the skin, but after the first ten minutes numbness, brought on by the cold, seemed to allay the discomfort, except for the face and eyes.

It was only possible to catch sight of anything occasionally and even then it was difficult to distinguish at once whether it was a ship or just another dark wave. We sighted the convoy eventually and were overhauling it fast when the watch was relieved.

After such a watch breakfast should have been a pleasure, but the disgust in Jim's face when he brought it from the galley dashed our fond hopes. He dumped on the table a large kit of something hot which looked like granulose custard. He flung down beside it an unappealing lump of raw bacon.

The war with the cook had continued apace since we put to sea and our relations with the galley had not been improved when, a few days before, the kettle in which he boiled his barley concoction and its contents had disappeared overnight. The culprit could have been anyone of us, but I strongly suspected the Marine Sergeant who had earlier expressed the opinion that with so much water under our keel cooks were easily disposed of.

Whilst I did not imagine he would go that far, I had every reason to believe he could have made the symbolic gesture. He had been looking rather pleased with himself the following day. The mixture before us could well have been part of the cook's retaliation, but perhaps I was wrong. When I tried it I found it consisted of some kind of ground cereal, unusual but palatable.

The lump of cold bacon, which might have been acceptable if boiled or baked or even sliced, was a definite affront. Jim and I settled for some tinned pilchards from our emergency supply which, as time went on, was to become a regular standby. Eric fortified himself on the cook's bread which was beyond criticism and our ample supply of jam.

The convoy had altered course again and the weather was moderating rapidly. We were sad to see that the *EMPIRE DACE*, the vehicle ferry, was missing. She had probably been hove-to during the height of the storm and we hoped she had survived and guessed that one of the escort ships would now be looking for her.

On the whole the vessels around us seemed to have weathered it well, but we noticed that the *PENSHURST* had two of her liferafts missing and other signs of damage to her deck gear.

The abatement in the weather brought with it some swift recoveries among the crew, but Ginger, staunchly carrying on, was still trying to hold down his diet of toast. George, the deck boy from Cardiff, was at last able to quit his bunk and with all the enthusiasm of the reborn set about cleaning up the shambles in our quarters. Though we were probably in the most dangerous stage of our Atlantic leg there was a distinct rise in spirits, helped later in the day by the sight of a larger, faster convoy obviously bound for the Gibraltar Strait.

The next day as we approached The Rock with everyone on the alert we met a heavily escorted convoy of fast transports, some of them recognisable as popular pre-war passenger liners in spite of their grey paint, no doubt bound for Britain to pick up another load of servicemen.

Passing into the Strait in the afternoon we met another convoy of large cargo ships, now unladen and making their run for home. If we had not known it before we now had no lingering doubts that we formed part of the war's largest sea-borne invasion force to date.

We anchored off The Rock in a bay packed with ships awaiting orders or taking their turn to replenish fuel and stores. There was a general atmosphere of expectation, but for a few hours we relaxed.

Only Jim and the older Jacob seemed cogitative. They had been in deep discussion with some of the firemen and greasers who occupied the accommodation across the alleyway on the port side of the fo'c'sle. They had realised, shrewdly, that any gossip emanating from the engine room would, for relevant technological reasons, be most likely to have a basis in fact.

In that department, they discovered, it was already anticipated that the *ODYSSEUS* would not be quitting the Mediterranean - the

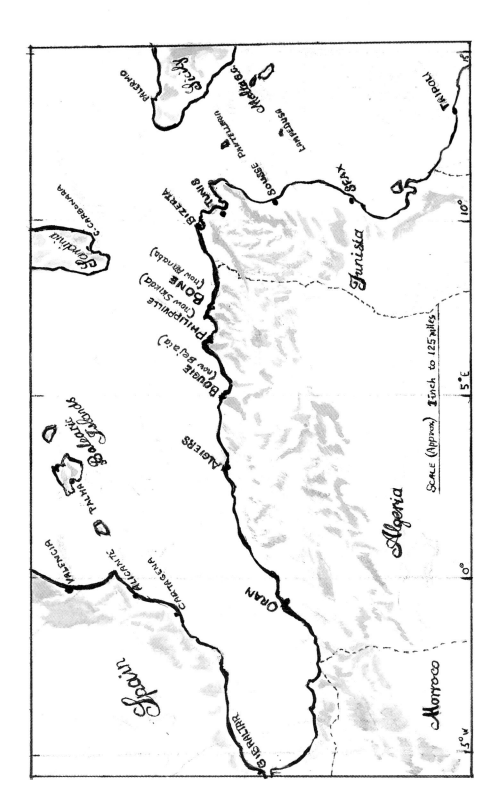

SCALE (Approx.) 1 inch to 125 miles

Middellandse Zee they called it - for as many months as her mechanical efficiency, or the enemy, allowed.

There was a more sobering logic in Jim's further appraisal. It was barely three months since the widely publicised "Pedestal" convoy had sailed through the Strait bound for beleaguered Malta. For most of that voyage, almost as far as Cape Bon in Tunisia, they had a protective screen of two battleships, three aircraft carriers, many cruisers and several flotillas of destroyers, yet nine of them had been sunk and only four of their cargoes delivered.

The North African coast, with its many vital ports, lying far beyond Algiers was no less open to such determined attack. It made perfect sense to spread the supply load among as many small vessels as possible, Jim thought.

By such piecemeal dispersal a much larger proportion of incoming cargoes, discharged from the larger and less expendable ships, could be relayed safely to the forward bases where they were most needed. It was not unreasonable to suppose, he argued, that the loss of any ships such as ours would be considered minor setbacks as they could be more easily replaced.

His logistics were difficult to fault, but we rather hoped Jim's prognostications were merely a rare glimpse of his gloomier side.

SERULA - a post-War picture of one of the survivors from the
British contingent in the conscripted fleet of small deep-sea steamers.
(Courtesy of FotoFlite)

CHAPTER THREE

We weighed anchor the next morning and idled impatiently in Algeciras Bay awaiting our turn to go alongside. Those gunners who had been lucky in the draw and hoped to enjoy a brief spell ashore had turned to in smart array.

Sergeant Bunce who had hinted at such an outing the previous evening, once the weaponry had been overhauled and cleaned to his satisfaction, sunned himself on the boat deck and wore an enigmatic smile.

In the event whatever bunkers we required we were given little time to make good the depletion. We had barely made fast and the coal had only just started to come aboard, when the signal came to cast off and it became evident that the ships of our onward bound convoy were preparing to leave.

The disappointment among the gunners who saw their jaunt ashore so ruthlessly snatched away was forgotten soon after, super-seded by general joy and surprise, at the sight of the *EMPIRE DACE* which had caught up with us. It remained a puzzle as to why a vessel so obviously designed for more sheltered voyaging had been included in our expedition. We were to find out in due course and to admire her vital role.

It took some time to assemble the convoy, which now included a much wider variety of ships, and we did not get away, heading east from that northern Pillar of Hercules, until the afternoon. The escort consisting mainly of anti-submarine sloops, trawlers and destroyers, was impressive.

We guessed that a proportion of U-boats from the Atlantic hunting ground had already passed into the Mediterranean, using the inward current to glide through with electric motors shut down, and the unique temperature layers to, hopefully, deflect any searching asdic probes. It would explain to some extent their missing attention to us on the voyage down.

The convoy did not form into columns until night was approaching and we were well beyond the narrow gateway to the Middle Sea. The weather was cloudy but the sea was not high and the visibility was good. If we had been alert on previous watches the conditions now helped us to be even more so, but there was no alarm through the night and the next day dawned warm and clear.

Though we had so far only seen the distant coast of Spain we were now certain we were heading for Algiers and some port beyond. Some of the ships in the convoy were bound for Oran, a normal steaming distance of some 230 sea miles, but we were taking the longest route and did not expect them to leave us until the following day.

Before nightfall we had altered course and by the early morning the far peaks of the Atlas Range were showing beyond the hazy coastline. Shortly before breakfast those ships bound for Oran, which was now safely in Allied control after fierce initial resistance by the French, broke away to head inshore.

The horizon cleared quickly under the warmth of the rising sun and, just as swiftly it seemed, was dispelled any remaining tension from the night watches. It was with some satisfaction however, that we noted the speedy return of the escort ships which had shepherded our departing consorts in.

The news we had picked up at Gibraltar had been on the whole encouraging. The assault convoys for the three pronged attack on the major ports of Oran, Algiers and Casablanca, codenamed Operation Torch, had been secretly approaching their objectives under cover of darkness whilst we were still in the North Atlantic pondering our future and the purpose of our mission.

The first two armadas of assault ships and fast troopships, in company with powerful units of the Royal Navy, had sailed from Britain. The third invasion force had sailed directly from the United States. At Algiers and Oran the element of surprise had brought a swift achievement of the objective.

At Oran it had taken somewhat longer, perhaps because of the bitter memories of July 1940 when a reluctant, but determined British Navy had shelled French warships at their base at Mers el Kiber.

At Casablanca there had been greater difficulties. The high surf on the Atlantic beaches impeded the early landings and Vichy warships, including the battleship *JEAN BART*, had to be overpowered by the U.S. Navy. It was two days after the main footholds had been established at Algiers that Admiral Darlan broadcast his orders from that city calling on all the local French forces to cease fire.

We had been en route for Gibraltar whilst such dramatic events were taking place and had heard only briefly of the Axis forces' reactions to such sudden and strategic Allied enterprise. Yet no-one aboard doubted that in the intervening days they would have responded

24

swiftly and violently, particularly with their powerful concentration of warplanes which had given them the air advantage over those waters for so long.

The heartening news we had picked up at Gibraltar was that, within hours of the occupation of Algiers, Hurricane and Spitfire fighters had been flown in to captured airfields to begin restoring the balance. Future air cover was very much in our minds.

Any complacency engendered by such seeds of optimism was, in the afternoon, suddenly put back on hold. Soon after the sun had passed its zenith the hydrophonic thud of exploding depth-charges reverberated along our bottom plates with the resounding force of a foundry hammer.

It was followed immediately by our U-boat alarm signal and anxious eyes searched the shimmering waters within our periphery.

It was an emergency of short duration, just a reminder in fact that from then on no part of our stay in those contested waters was going to be without its instant menace, night or day, for months to come.

If the escort's sonic probe had in fact detected a predatory submarine, its Commander must have got the message because we were not troubled further on our voyage to Algiers. Though most of those aboard had heard, often enough, the detonation of depth-charges against ship's bilges, the change in attitude was at once perceptible.

Sergeant Bunce monopolised the port Oerlikon gun, scanning the sky with professional detachment, but with all the eagerness of a man impatient to demonstrate his skill. In the amateur field it was interesting to note that the Bo'sun too seemed keen to establish his proficiency. He spent the remaining hours of daylight hovering near the twin-Marlin, frequently taking over other crew members' gun watches.

Everyone now had their lifejackets and helmets at hand and when Jim came off watch that evening he did not turn in at once. He sat smoking for a long time and eventually went to sleep on a bench. The fo'c'sle could never have been the easiest place to evacuate in an emergency with its cramped space, narrow alleyway and heavy steel door.

For all but those whose duties lay in the stokehold or engine room, being on watch suddenly seemed infinitely preferable to a warm bunk and for reasons no one discussed.

The engineers, donkeyman and greasers, and the firemen and trimmers, worked four hour watches and went about their business with no visible display of concern, but they would have been less than human to have harboured no secret anxiety about maintaining steam in the bowels of what was, potentially, a floating bomb.

The convoy altered course after daybreak and soon we got our first sight of Algiers. Rising above a broad, grey frieze of anchored ships of many types and sizes, that ancient base of the Barbary pirates looked white and clean in the strong sunlight. Its modern buildings of French influence overlooking the vast waterfront blended well with its picturesque background.

In harsh contrast the astonishing assembly of ships, which we were about to join in the wide bay, formed a spectacle which would have made Barbarossa himself quail. There were cruisers, destroyers, armed trawlers, minesweepers and fleet auxiliaries, large passenger liners converted for trooping, Channel ferries transformed into assault landing vessels and a multitude of cargo ships, large and small.

Some of the latter were unladen awaiting convoy out, but the majority, like ourselves, were waiting to be discharged or to join other convoys destined for smaller ports much further east. Inside the port could be seen some of the larger cargo ships being urgently unloaded and many French ships in peacetime livery, now separated for the duration of the war from their home port of Marseilles.

After dropping both anchors in a position as convenient to the port entrance as that great congregation of ships would allow, we launched our motor lifeboat. Soon after the Captain appeared, dressed for official business, and quickly embarked taking with him the assistant steward who knew Algiers well from peacetime voyaging and the young assistant cook who needed dental treatment.

The two Jacobs who were in charge of the boat waved to us a derisory farewell as they headed for the shore, knowing the mate would find us plenty to do aboard. He immediately gave me the job of taking soundings for it was as well to know how much water we had under our keel.

He spoke of sudden gales and seemed anxious about the nature of the holding ground, keenly examining the base of the lead whenever I coiled in the line to examine the evidence it held of the sea floor's composition. He seem satisfied, but it was a reasonable precaution hemmed in as we were by so many ships.

The important job we had to tackle was our washing. There had been little opportunity to attempt it until then. By the time our boat returned the results of our industry were fluttering from many lines strung across the foredeck.

Whatever news the Captain had brought back was not passed on directly and we saw no particular significance in the order to lay out the deck hoses as the sun sank. It seemed an elementary precaution.

Gun watches were maintained and those not on anchor watch turned in cautiously that night, partly dressed and with helmets and lifejackets at hand. From what we had seen Algiers was well protected from sea attack and in the sky we had not seen so much as a reconnaissance plane, yet there was the strong feeling that the pattern of enemy retaliation might soon emerge.

Its demonstration came that night in a crescendo of gunfire which almost beat the clarion summons of the alarm bell. It was opened by those naval ships with heavier ack-ack guns on the seaward fringes of the anchorage and was rapidly taken up by hundreds of other weapons, of a dozen recognisable varieties, manned by gunners in lesser warships and in the extensive fleet of merchant ships great and small.

From its deadly crackle and thunder one could pick out the heartening bark of naval pom-poms, the rapid thump of the Bofors and the steady discharge of manually served 12-pounders. The ear shattering tumult seemed instantly more bearable because of the simultaneous pyrotechnics display for which it formed the symphony. No fireworks presentation, however grand or well orchestrated, could have matched the effect of so many streaking tracers.

From more than one direction came the sinister swoosh of newly introduced rocket weapons whose explosive charges burst in regular patterns high in that pitch black arena.

I made first for the boat deck and was not greatly surprised to find the Bo'sun already installed behind our puny Marlins. Though it was virtually impossible to detect the direction of any engine sounds in our vicinity he was firing steady bursts from his twin barrels.

It was a long time before the first real break in what proved to be a series of closely spaced attacks and in that lull the Marine Sergeant called down from the bridge for the Bo'sun to save his ammunition and not to fire unless we were closely attacked. Sergeant Bunce had been blazing away in various directions and soon resumed doing so, pouring 20mm Oerlikon shells at planes he alone seemed able to detect.

The army gunner Jim Nevarde, whom we called The Bombardier, was more thrifty with his ammunition I noted and shared some concern with the others that supplies might quickly run out if raids of such intensity became a regular experience. We were all soon to become proficient at manhandling the heavy boxes of shells and helping with the careful task of loading the H.E. and tracer shells into the cylindrical magazines in correct proportion.

So far we had only heard one bomb bursting in the water near us and our main concern was to avoid the rain of hot metal fragments from the defensive barrage, which clanged on our metal decks or hissed and splashed in the sea around. Eventually there came a longer lull and then a signal which gave the "All Clear".

Sleep did not come easily afterwards and when it did was abruptly interrupted by the arrival of another wave of bombers which were greeted in the same warm style in the hours before dawn. They did not trouble us for long and were no doubt relieved to get back to their base in time for an early breakfast.

As an interruption to what we might expect from now on it had been a lesson in collective security and might even have been comforting if we could have relied on always being in such vast company.

Daylight revealed few signs of destruction or damage to our gathering, but later it was noticed that a cruiser appeared to have suffered from a near miss, and we were puzzled for a time by the odd trim of a large, single funnelled Cunarder, the *SCYTHIA* I think, which we later heard had been the victim of an aerial torpedo. There was no report of any ship having been sunk.

The raid had brought a change in our habits and all those with no duties to perform took to their bunks to stock up on sleep in preparation for what the night would bring. Such wisdom was endorsed when the enemy returned in force. If anything the barrage was more intense and flares dropped by some of the raiders added dramatically to the Wagnerian contest.

Early on I was able to establish prior claim to the twin-Marlin in the gun box abaft the funnel, which was a victory of sorts and immediately benefitted from a new system of gunnery control devised by Sergeant Bunce. From the high pitch of the attackers' engines it seemed they were pressing their attentions more closely and, from his wing of the bridge, that veteran warrior quickly identified their approach and gave the orders to fire.

SCYTHIA (20,000 grt) - Veteran Cunarder serving as troop transport which was crippled by aerial torpedoes off Algiers on November 23, 1942. Built in 1920 she survived the war and was scrapped in 1958.

Retaliating however blindly, was infinitely preferable to standing around and I soon had to reload. There came one moment of premature triumph when a tongue of flame rewarded our hopeful concentration of tracers high over our port quarter. The Sergeant and the gunner in the after gun box were also firing in that direction, but at the first flicker I was prepared to claim it if only for the honour of the amateur side.

Yet even in that moment of sudden elation I realised something was wrong. The flames spread and hung there like a captive beacon at one o'clock high. The realisation that some ship's barrage balloon, negligently left aloft at nightfall, had paid the penalty cancelled all claims immediately. The Sergeant who had started to shout something though better of it and never mentioned the matter later.

There were still no orders for us the next day and we stood to at dusk ready for a third night of violent attention. When it came it was longer sustained, but no more successful. The impressive sight and sound of so many ships fighting back at enemies we could only hear was not so much an exciting experience as an interruption we could well do without.

It had served the useful purpose of streamlining our defensive efficiency for what that was worth and it had instilled some confidence in the crew in our ability to cope with determined attack. It was clear we were going to have to live with the expectation of hearing the alarm bell frequently and its initial shock would never again be quite so startling.

The knowledge that if any one of the ships laden with ammunition or petrol, or both, had been hit in the last three nights, the outcome might have been devastating, seemed good enough reason for getting to sea. Word of such a move would certainly have pleased us, but we sensed something other than dilatory organisation was causing the delay.

The mate's earlier concern over the weather was not unfounded. It had turned colder and quite suddenly became more like a November day back in Britain, with a blustery wind which strengthened quickly bringing white crests to the mounting waves. As a precaution the boat we had alongside was sent ashore in the care of the two Jacobs.

By the early evening a gale was blowing with every sign that it would reach storm force. The mate called us to pay out another shackle on each cable and we felt confident in our ground tackle. If we had any concern it was that some other ship might drag down on us during the night.

We were relaxing in the fo'c'sle thinking about turning in when I heard a muffled crack from the deck above and taking a torch went up to investigate. Everything looked in order, but when I felt the cable in the port hawsepipe I realised at once that it had parted somewhere and was hanging loose. For any such heavy, studded link to have snapped was a grim indication of the pressure of the wind.

While someone roused the mate, Joe and I searched the darkness to estimate, if we could, how quickly the ship might be dragging, but it seemed that our starboard anchor was still holding. First we paid out more cable to relieve the extra weight on it whilst the engine room was alerted to get some way on her.

It was an emergency brought on by our natural enemy, the storm, but there was no way in which we could head directly for open water to ride it out.

As soon as we had got our remaining anchor in, and recovered what was left of our broken cable, there began the intensely nerve-racking job of threading our way safely through that mass of blacked-out shipping to seek more sheltered water.

The white crests came to our aid more than once as they broke against the hidden stems of the ships around us and flashed their foaming trails against dark hulls. In contrast with the excitements of previous nights it seemed no less harrowing. Indeed any flare from a Junkers or Heinkel might at times have lightened our predicament.

After what seemed like hours of backing and filling, and creeping timorously through that silent maze, Captain Ruig ordered our port anchor to be let go. Even Jim, who had been at the wheel for much of the time, found it entirely reasonable to double the anchor watch until daylight brought its welcome relief.

In fact, its first streaks brought some surprises for we found ourselves lying as near to the port entrance as we could possibly be without encroaching upon its access. As it grew lighter we could see that we had been luckier than some for, over to the east of the bay, an assault ship appeared to be ashore and it seemed at least one other vessel would need refloating.

Soon there came another surprise to make us shrug off our mainly sleepless night. We got a signal to enter the port. Shorthanded as we were with two sailors already ashore, it took us no time at all to get up our one anchor and prepare to go alongside.

Any hopes that we were about to discharge our cargo were soon banished. For once we found ourselves in touch with a source of information, both reliable and up-to-date. The men of the Royal Engineers Dock Companies, who had been a vital part of the spear-head of operation "Torch", cheerfully filled us in with the latest news soon after we were tied up.

They had obviously not had an easy time and were still living rough, sleeping on the hard concrete floors of quayside warehouses which gave them some protection from the bombing. They were the real thing, experienced dockers from British ports, mainly London and Liverpool and such north-east towns as Grimsby.

They had joined Territorial units in peacetime and now found themselves importantly employed and very much in the front line. The only local supplement to their basic army rations had been tangerine oranges and what they craved most of all was bread. It was one thing our cook produced in abundance and their briefing did not go unrewarded.

Along with the other small ships we would be taking our cargo further east to one or other of the smaller ports where subsequent landings had been made. The original hopes of securing Bizerta, the important French naval base in Tunisia to the west of Cape Bon, had been dashed by the arrival of a powerful enemy presence during the protracted negotiations between the Allies and the French.

It had created a line of enemy resistance running south from the coast in the vicinity of Cape Serrat, not many miles within the Tunisian border. The furthermost Allied supply port close to that forward line was Bone, some 270 miles east of Algiers. Near it, in its own bay to the west was the smaller port of Philippeville and halfway back along the coast lay Bougie.

Hopes that the once efficient railway service across Algiers would prove a useful supply system for the Sixth Army's thrust had been as much a disappointment as the road routes, and the three ports had now become vital bridgeheads. The enemy had been swift to realise that also and the dockers in khaki, who had friends in other units there, had no better comfort to offer us than their best wishes for a quick turn round.

Few of the crew got beyond the dock area. We had fresh water to take in and our lifeboat to recover and hoist inboard. The Captain went in search of some spare anchor cable to replace those shackles we had lost. Mercifully that night the enemy left us in peace.

Captain Ruig had tracked down some cable of the right size and from early next morning until almost sunset we laboured like a chain gang, first getting our spare anchor free of the clamps which had become almost welded to it over the years, then laying out the 15-fathom shackles of heavy chain on the quay for tarring and marking and joining up.

Urgency had by that time become such a part of daily routine it never occurred to any of us that we were working against time. I was having a leisurely wash when I heard the Bo'sun calling and the telegraph ringing the standby. Within minutes it seemed we were casting off, our screw was turning again and the long harbour mole was slipping astern.

Any thoughts we had of returning to the anchorage passed from our minds when we noticed other ships also on the move and heading for sea. The Bo'sun, who had just come from the bridge, said in confidential tones: "We're off to Philippeville." I feel sure it came as a relief to most of us to learn that we were at last on the most important leg of our outward voyage.

CHAPTER FOUR

Our departure had either been a sudden decision strategically taken or it indicated a degree of secrecy by which we could expect to be constantly in the dark over future sailing schedules. It had meant us leaving with two of the crew still ashore.

The assistant steward and one of the greasers had not made it back in time and would be badly missed by those whose work load was now increased. It was easy to anticipate that, from now on, Captain Ruig would be frugal in rationing any shore leave when the opportunity offered.

Such thoughts were fleeting. The weather had changed for the better. Indeed it was a superb night. But for the circumstances and the nature of our mission it would have been a pleasure taking the first spell at the wheel. I was sharing the watch with Jim and the Bo'sun and, but for the sound of planes overhead and the rumble of gunfire soon afterwards from far astern, it passed quietly.

The thought that Algiers was having another noisy night bolstered our feeling of relief to be out of that target area and at sea again with room to manoeuvre and the comforting concealment of the night.

If we had any concern it was over our position in the convoy. We were the last ship in the outermost file, vulnerable to opportunist attack, particularly from the air. The consoling thought was that when daylight came with its usual flag signals from the Commodore ship, we would not have to repeat those hoists. The single answering pennant would suffice.

As far as we had been able to see there were no more than twenty ships in the formation, but it was difficult in the darkness to assess the strength of the escort. I was on watch again at 8.00am with the two Jacob's and was heartened to note there were two or three destroyers in the offing with one or two sloops among the smaller warships in closer attendance.

But for their presence and our own orderly array, the wider scene would have made a compelling poster for the long banished Mediterranean cruise traffic. Where the sea was not transformed into molten silver its shade captured the cloudless, cobalt immensity above.

Having been relieved at the wheel I was admiring the effect with my Scheveningen shipmate, the young Jacob, when an object on the port bow caught our eyes. As we steamed up on it we looked down on an enemy airman who would fly no more. His parachute was still attached and his boots, shimmering in the sunlight, shone with a gloss only we could admire.

Jim, who had just come up to relieve the look-out, was gently rebuked by the second mate for expressing the hope that all the Axis airmen he saw would be as harmless.

Not many minutes later, with appetites sharpened by the five-hours watch, we were about to attack the cook's unmemorable plat du jour when the alarm bell deafened us. Its earnest clamour temporarily drowned the hostile engine beat which had already alerted those on the bridge to an impending attack.

By the time we had gained the foredeck the presence of the approaching aircraft was clearly visible. Sweeping towards us from far out on the port bow was a formation of Heinkels, torpedo planes without a doubt, flying at mast height and widely spread out to confuse the defence.

I counted seven or eight in that split-second glance, but there were probably more. They seemed to be hanging there in that instant like some malignant mobile, swinging menacingly against the placid blue.

Guns opened up from those escort ships ahead of the convoy and on its port flank, but their altitude and disposition made them no easy target, and they were still too far beyond the range of our weapons for any real concentration of fire.

As I reached the midship section two of them broke away, coming in at mast-height in our direction. Then, as our guns and those of other ships in the column ahead of us opened fire, they banked away.

With a cockney irony David Garrick could never have intended when he wrote the lyrics for Heart of Oak, one of our gunners broke the tension by bursting into song. "Come cheer up my lads..." was as far as he got before his voice was drowned by the rising pitch of a Heinkel's twin engines as the first plane returned to the attack.

It was again turning towards us, followed closely by its neighbour making a broader sweep, and was levelling out with the clear intention of attempting our destruction. Because of its beam approach we could only bring two Oerlikons to bear and they opened up, supported by the twin-Marlin, in withering response, but without noticeably deflecting the pilot from his purpose.

The speed of its approach and the glare of the sun beyond its sinister shadow made it difficult to spot the launch of any torpedoes. Time had stopped still, but it could only have been seconds before it was banking steeply and the 20mm cannon shells were flicking along its underside, now significantly devoid of both missiles.

Moments later the second Heinkel, its shrill engines racing, was exposing its belly as it sped up our port side and got our concentrated fire. There followed a moment of fleeting satisfaction as we saw them head away with one trailing smoke. Then came a feeling of relief not untinged with foreboding as we heard the steering quadrant's rattle and thud as the helm went hard-over.

The tension was far from over. Indeed the drama was only beginning. As *ODYSSEUS*' bow began to answer, all eyes switched instinctively back to the water. Even with the helm hard-a-port there was a maddening dignity about her swing. Straining eyes picked out the faint trail of the approaching torpedo, only breaking the mesmeric spell to glance in silent prayer at the quickening counter-movement of our turning stem.

From the boatdeck, just below the bridge, I watched its now clear trail heading straight for the bow, and gripped the rail as its vertex was blotted out by the bulk of the fo'c'slehead. Seconds later it was a welcome sight as it appeared on our starboard bow heading for the distant shore. Suddenly, to all who breathed freely again, it had become a mere curiosity disappearing into an empty seascape.

Only the gunner in the after gun box saw its twin. He had watched it bearing down on us as all other eyes, apart from those, stoically engaged in the engine room and stokehold had been fixed on the bow. His shouting had not attracted much interest and in moments of silent suspense he had watched its track enter the swirl of our wake as it too so narrowly missed its target.

Everyone had been so intent on our own problems at the rear of the convoy we had been paying scant attention to the fortunes of our consorts. As we were congratulating ourselves on our good fortune the full horror of what might have been erupted just ahead.

The ship we had been following in the outside line was a Norwegian named the *SELBO*, a vessel of the same vintage and size as ours. We had been anchored within easy hailing distance of her at Algiers and we knew from her crew, who seemed quite philosophical about it, that she carried a cargo of canned aviation spirit.

36

Norwegian steamer SELBO (1,778 grt) became blazing inferno and sank following torpedo plane attack whilst carrying case petrol, in convoy with ODYSSEUS off Cape Cavallo, Algeria (November 28, 1942)
(Courtesy of World Ship Society)

Now the elation and relief at our deliverance was forgotten in a flash as we saw her transformed into a blazing inferno, with a shocking abruptness only horror movies could strive to present.

Only Jim van Ommeren, our lookout man on the monkey island above the bridge, had seen the impact of the torpedo as it exploded against the plates of her No. 3 hold. The conflagration was immediate and within seconds she had disappeared, obliterated by a broad column of flame which instantly rose mast-high, its vermilion changing rapidly to deep crimson as it mounted to a height of more than two hundred feet.

This immense pillar of flame which, in the still air, remained absolutely vertical, was capped with a mushroom of dense black smoke which quickly took over, descending like a vast cylindrical curtain to meet the sea. Beneath its fringes the flames leaped in an ever widening circle as if to mock any possible escape from the stricken ship.

We could feel the intense heat on our faces as we drew nearer and hot greasy smuts began to blacken our decks and paintwork. Already we had cut the lashings on the scrambling nets on our starboard side and flung their folds outboard.

Our action was instinctive and backed by the forlorn hope that somewhere on the fringe of that obscene pyre some strong swimmer might still be alive however badly burned, but we also knew the rules. Ships in convoy did not break ranks, however merciful the mission.

There was also the important consideration of our own volatile load. The heat was intense and it came as no surprise when Captain Ruig altered course to give those spreading flames a wide berth. It was some consolation to see one of the escorting trawlers speeding up from astern on what still seemed a hopeless rescue attempt.

As we watched her nosing in to that infernal circle we feared for her safety too and admired the courage of her crew. It was only as we drew ahead that we saw there was still hope. The bow of the doomed ship emerged for a moment, starkly outlined against the ruby glow. Jim pointed suddenly to a dark object far beyond it and we recognised it as a blackened boat in which we counted six or seven men.

It seemed unbelievable that any boat could have got away from that fiery cataclysm and we marvelled that at least one of those huddled figures was seen to move. By that time there was plenty for us to do. Ammunition boxes had to be opened and magazines reloaded ready for any further attack. It was a job for all spare hands as weapons were overhauled.

After so much adrenalin had flowed, everyone seemed to have become very quiet, no doubt occupied with their own thoughts. Quite soon though it seemed all had something to say. As we greased the cannon shells before they were loaded I heard the Marine Sergeant opining with some authority that his plane which had been seen trailing smoke must have crashed in the sea.

His use of that possessive term prompted Jack Ridler, the Radio Officer, to point our that as an independent witness he considered the gunner on the poop had most claim to it. Sparks, we soon realised, was a stickler for fair play. Sergeant Bunce, whilst justifiably maintaining a share in any fate which might have befallen our first attacker, switched smartly to a detailed review of his assault on the second Heinkel which had almost certainly torpedoed the Norwegian.

By that time all the planes had vanished leaving only that lurid spire astern of us as evidence of their attack. The Sergeant's words were momentarily drowned by the sound of fighter aircraft, which passed over our wake in fast pursuit moments later. They got a slightly ironic cheer, but it was good to see they were about.

Twenty minutes later we could have wished they were still around. From ahead and from on high, came the distant sound of much deeper aircraft noises and the alarm bell sounded once more. Before we could see them we knew from the volume that there were a great many more of them.

They were coming towards us on much the same course as the Heinkels must have used for their approach, but were still too far away to be positively identified. Ted Maloney, the shortest of our Maritime Regiment detachment, who was manning our after gun was generally accepted as our aircraft recognition expert.

He was a Londoner from Battersea, a man of impassive disposition with a dead-pan style of humour. As he stood on the edge of his gun position shading his eyes, he counted them aloud until he got to thirteen. The suspense was too much for Sergeant Bunce who shouted from his wing of the bridge: "Tell us whose they are!"

But Maloney was not to be hurried. "They're four engined jobs," he announced and then, after a long pause in which the suspense reached its highest pitch, he gave a pawky smile and calmly declared: "They're Fortresses." How long it had taken him to recognise them was his secret, but in the immediate wave of relief, and perhaps because we suddenly realised that they might have been bombing enemy airfields, all suspicion was forgotten.

Soon afterwards the large procession of bombers, keeping well away from the convoy, altered their course for the coast. For the remainder of that afternoon those off watch showed little inclination to claim their bunks. When nightfall came most were still watching the sky or gazing back at the awesome manifestation of our first close encounter, still visible on the western skyline.

It was midnight when we broke away from the convoy and, with another Norwegian ship, were led through what we presumed to be a swept channel to anchor in a broad bay outside the port of Philippeville. The pilot who came out told us that an alert was on, but no enemy activity developed and, in the early hours, we moved inside and moored to a buoy in the outer harbour.

Those off watch got a few hours sleep, but most of the ship's company were awake soon after sunrise to take a first look at the place where, we hoped, we might be quickly relieved of the cargo we were delivering after a voyage of some 2,000 miles. The dramatic events which had changed that sunlit haven into a front line bridgehead had left their mark.

Though the town, from what we could see of it, appeared to have escaped well from the regular air raids which had followed the Allied occupation, the port area showed many signs of enemy attention. From the first light it had been noisy with khaki-clad activity as dockside cranes and ship's winches competed to feed the constantly moving queues of army vehicles.

Dispersing the off-loaded supplies of ammunition, petrol and provisions before the enemy returned was clearly a priority, but the mounds of capricious cargo stacked along the quays indicated the herculean extent of that awesome task. For the time being we felt happier to remain outside.

Not that our mooring beyond the quays distanced us very much from the heart of that activity for it was a compact port, cradled in a natural inlet enclosed by rocky hills. If we had any doubt about its dangerous location the evidence of a recent enemy success lay, half-submerged, not far from us.

Though it was no real surprise to see a ship so violently overwhelmed in those surroundings, it came as something of a shock when she was soon identified by one of the Dutch crew as a vessel they all knew well. She was the *AURORA*, of Amsterdam, belong to the same company.

She was larger than the *ODYSSEUS* and a couple of years older, but in maritime affections she was a close relative. Some of our crew had served in her and most of her ship's company had been friends or acquaintances. Their fate became a matter of immediate concern until it was learned from her mate, who was temporarily stranded in the port and soon came aboard, that no lives had been lost.

He had once been erste stuurman in the *ODYSSEUS* and held no false hopes for our easy future, an opinion supported only too well by the forlorn sight of his own ship which had been the victim of heavy air attack five nights before, fortunately after she had discharged her cargo. It had been similar in content to ours and had been loaded in Port Talbot from where she had sailed a few days before us.

Because of the large number of ships and the shortage of quays and an unexpected delay in securing the port she had been kept waiting to unload for some days.

She had been waiting for a convoy to return to Algiers for another load when the attack began and, at its height, she had been hit by a bomb in the forward section, quickly settling by the bow. Her sorry presence and his account somewhat dented the growing faith in

AURORA (1,700 grt) - She became the first K.N.S.M. victim of the enemy's fierce retaliation from the air when she was bombed and sunk with her Dutch ensign still flying at Philippeville on November 24, 1942.

(Courtesy of Nedlloyd)

our own good luck and there were not a few who envied him his pending departure.

Fortunately the sun was shining, and all day and through the night no sinister drone disturbed our peace. The next morning I went ashore with the younger Jacob. There were things some of the crew were getting short of and we hoped to find them in the shops near the quays. It was not very promising.

Philippeville would have been a pleasant, even prosperous, colonial town in normal times with its colonnaded pavements and cool shadows, but now its shops held little for any customer to linger over. There was an air of extended deprivation about them which had little to do with the sudden involvement of warring factions. France's subjugated neutrality had clearly been a meagre option.

There were oranges, particularly tangerines, in abundance and we filled a seabag with them. We were also able to buy razor blades and there was a plentiful supply of best Algerian briar pipes, but not much else. As we were thinking of exploring further the siren wailed.

The Islamic and Berber population very sensibly faded away rapidly, but the French shopkeepers delayed seeking shelter long enough to close the shutters on their windows before disappearing in various directions, leaving Jacob and me in the otherwise deserted street. We decided to keep on walking until we could see the harbour.

A lone plane, probably a Junkers 88, came in over the hills behind the town to be met by stream of tracers from the ships in port. The sight of the *ODYSSEUS* in action was an inspiring experience we were glad not to have missed. For her small armament she seemed to be putting on a very impressive display.

The attempt at surprise was smartly frustrated and we saw the plane fly off beyond a headland apparently damaged in one engine. Later we heard it had crashed in the sea and the gunner who claimed it was our own Jim Nevarde of the Maritime Regiment. When we got back aboard there was an air of jubilation which put everyone in a braver mood for what was to come.

CHAPTER FIVE

That night the enemy returned in force and we got the full flavour of what it meant to be caught loitering on that stretch of the coast. Each wave of attack was signalled on the port siren a few minutes in advance, usually just as those off duty were dropping off to sleep again.

There could be no doubting the enemy's determination to make Philippeville untenable in one way or another, either by blasting its supply ships, blowing up the ammunition and petrol dumps on its quays, or by enforcing the collapse of its defenders and workforce through sheer lack of sleep. That's how it seemed.

The assaults were of fairly short duration, but spaced at such intervals as to keep everyone on their toes from before midnight until dawn. The thick smokescreen, which was laid every time and which had us all coughing and wheezing with smarting eyes long after our visitors had gone, was another factor we had not reckoned with.

It was released from canisters and was so intense, it made breathing difficult, severely impaired close vision, and was probably toxic to a degree no lung specialist would have found acceptable.

One obvious drawback for those gunners with keen eyesight was that, whilst it screened us from predatory selection, it cancelled any chance of getting a visual bearing in the light of any flares or against the background of stars. We had seen no evidence of any searchlights.

It was clear that those in charge of the port's defences believed in the comparative effectiveness of that suffocating pall and probably considered its fumes a minor discomfort to the alternative of ships being targeted individually and, perhaps, they had a point.

Nevertheless, even with the support of the 40mm Bofors guns sited on the shore we could mass no barrage to match that of Algiers. In that confined space we could only think of our evil smelling cloak, which was blacker than the night, as a perfect marker for the enemy's bomb sights.

So far as I had seen there was no naval vessel in port larger than the armed trawler which had brought us in, but in the event we did not do badly. Among the larger ships unloading was an Ellerman cargo liner - the *CITY OF VENICE*, I think - which put up an impressive show.

Each raid began with the sound of planes circling the area and was quickly followed by the first of the attackers coming in at full throttle to drop its load along the line of the waterfront. Our streams of tracers emerging from the smoke must have had a daunting effect. As shore leave had been stopped when daylight came, we had no opportunity to inspect the results, but it was cheerfully reported from the shore as a goalless draw.

The anticipation of their return the next night made sleep a fitful pretence, but they left us alone and the following morning we were allowed to move into a harbour berth to take in fresh water. Seen at close hand, the contribution to the campaign being made by the army dock units increased our growing admiration for that branch of the Royal Engineers.

Running the gauntlet along the coast at least gave us the chance, for a while, of escaping that role of being sitting ducks. There could be no such release for them. It was their destiny to keep the port open and the cargoes moving at every cost. So much depended on it.

They were still quartered in the dock area, never getting very far from the highly explosive and inflammable tonnage they handled. In the absence of local food supplies they were living on compo rations. They gave us some for our own emergencies and were delighted when we provided them with fresh bread. The cook had also baked some for the crew of the naval trawler who presented us with some potatoes of which we were then short.

In Algiers Joe Stoakes had met among the dockers in battle-dress a Sergeant from Grimsby. In Philippeville he was able to pass on some messages to the man's brother in another R.E. port company. He told us of an incident during the landing there when he had seen an infantryman pause long enough to shoot down an attacking plane with a Bren gun, before turning and marching off up the street.

Those dockers were a reliable source of information. Having been drawn from most of Britain's major ports they had an avid interest in the careers of ships they had known in less destructive years. Though not surprised, we were awed by the numbers of famous pre-war passenger ships involved in the landings at those exposed easterly ports.

Bougie, in whose vicinity we had experienced our torpedo attack, seemed to have had the worst of it from the point of view of

VICEROY OF INDIA (19,648 grt) - P&O's stately turbo electric liner sunk by submarine torpedo north of Oran on November 11, 1942 whilst serving as an auxiliary transport in "Operation Torch" - the first of four ships of that fine fleet to be lost within five days.

(Courtesy of P&O)

losses, at a time when the enemy was recovering from its surprise and was desperately seeking to limit the Allies' success.

P&O Lines' *CATHAY* was the first victim. On 11th November, when people in Britain would be observing Armistice Day in memory of those who died in the First World War, the dive bombers came out of the clouds to blast in her engine room as she lay off the port disembarking troops. She was abandoned, but later erupted in flames after an explosion aboard.

The British India Lines' *KARANJA*, serving under the white ensign as an infantry landing ship, was soon afterwards hit by a stick of bombs and also went up in flames. The New Zealand Union Steamships Company's *AWATEA* was sunk by aerial torpedoes and bombs as she sailed away from Bougie, a fate which befell P&O's *NARKUNDA* three days later when she was dive-bombed leaving the port after landing her contingent.

Members of the R.E. port company arriving there in P&O's *STRATHNAVER* had witnessed much of it.

We were to learn subsequently that two other P&O Liners had been sunk in that short period whilst returning from that operation. One was the illustrious *VICEROY OF INDIA*, torpedoed between Algiers and Gibraltar, and the other was their fine new liner *ETTRICK* which was also lost to a U-boat soon after passing through the Strait.

For one company to lose four such important ships within four days was a grim indication of the scale and hazard of the operation. It was a high cost to pay, but left us with some small consolation in the *ODYSSEUS*' modest 1,100 gross tons. Being small was, perhaps, a bonus, a consideration to bolster our optimism.

The only cargo we had so far discharged was the large container of detonators which had been collected from us as we lay on the buoy, but whether that was out of some consideration for our safety or because of its urgent requirement, was not easy to fathom. Any hopes we held of unloading the rest of it were lost when the order came for us to move back to our previous mooring.

By way of diversion Jacob Harteveld and I sought permission to seek some dental attention and were soon ashore again armed with a written request from the master who seemed quite keen on exploring the local facilities. It turned out to be an education in more ways than one and a further introduction to military operations.

In most ports abroad we could have expected to be directed to a local dentist whose professional fees would be charged to the ship's account. Instead, probably for security reasons, we were handed hastily scrawled chits and sent along to a busy, makeshift surgery equipped and manned by the British Army.

Entering the commandeered premises with foreboding we viewed the efficiently regimented, conveyor belt process with rapidly dwindling enthusiasm. Soldiers from a variety of units were being slowly fed into the system for a preliminary examination, and the application of local anaesthetics, before returning to the outer waiting room to sit on long benches.

Our immediate reaction was to retire as gracefully as possible, but somehow under the circumstances it seemed cowardly and we fell into line. Unusually for a dentists' waiting room everyone seemed eager to talk, perhaps because of a shared anxiety that the pain deadener would have worn off before any of us reached the dental chairs the second time round.

There were men from units in the nearby hinterland obviously keen to get safely out of Philippeville without undue delay, certainly before dusk, and others from further afield where the enemy was being engaged on the ground, I imagined. They viewed their visit more philosophically, as a welcome interlude. Half an hour in their company brought us more information about the early fortunes of the campaign in the rough terrain to the east than we would otherwise have known.

When my turn came a shirt-sleeved officer of the Dental Corps wasted little time. He had strong forearms and no small talk and in two attempts removed my molar with a grunt of suppressed triumph. Before I could thank him a soldier had already taken my place. In the waiting room all the benches seemed to have filled up again.

The next day we went alongside to a discharging berth at a quay normally used for loading ore whose red dust lay heavily around the large bunkers in which it was piled. It was an export in decline. Only the imports of war mattered now. For the first time in weeks our hatch covers were peeled off and the long hatchboards and heavy steel beams were swung out to be stacked alongside the coamings.

In no time it seemed our compromising and combustible cargo was being transferred to the appropriate dumps along the harbour side with an industry heartening to watch. We were glad to see it go, but alarmed at the leaky state of many of the cans of petrol which formed such a large part of it. As they were stacked on the quay pools of aviation fuel formed round them like puddles after a rainstorm.

The P&O Liner CATHAY (15,225 grt) fell victim to enemy planes off Bougie on November 11, 1942. She blew up and sank the next day.
(Courtesy of Imperial War Museum - A12834)

The fumes were all pervading and we soon noted that none of the dockers spent long in that particular hold before coming up to clear their heads. The mate and the Bo'sun put their heads together to devise some kind of ventilating sail to be rigged as soon as that hold was cleared. By nightfall the ship was lighter by many hundred tons and the Sergeant in charge told us it might only take another three days.

That night the enemy returned and those who had no triggers to squeeze kept their fingers crossed. The smoke screen seemed thicker than ever and Sergeant Bunch with his usual initiative pulled on his gas respirator. In the end we all did, but later found that a damp cloth tied over the nose and mouth seemed more effective against such a burning fog.

It was a nasty raid with what seemed a large number of planes circling in the vicinity waiting their turn to make their bombing runs. Being now in the target centre we had to worry about the explosive possibilities of those mounds of cargo on the quay. The stacks of petrol were of particular concern and every preparation was made to move away as far as we could in the event of a blaze.

We heard bombs exploding on the quay and felt the blast and waited for the expected reaction which, miraculously, never came. Occasionally the ship lifted in the water as bombs exploded harmlessly on the harbour bed. When daylight came we gazed with astonishment on piles of earth thrown over some of the stacked munitions from bomb craters nearby.

There seemed to be only one casualty - the British ship *OUSEL*, which was considerably damaged, but was still afloat. We had not been aware of any cannon fire from the attackers, but it was rumoured that she had suffered some. The thought of some Junkers 88 emptying its guns into the smoke, as it came into the attack, was another torment to add to our growing list of fog induced apprehensions.

We had no raids again until our cargo was all ashore. The weather had turned damp and cloudy and might well have had something to do with it. The only excitement in that time was the sudden departure of a large merchant ship under orders to join a convoy bound from Bone to Algiers. She had to sail leaving some of her Liverpool crew ashore.

There were about fifteen of them and they were not at all pleased to find themselves, through no fault of their own, homeless on such an inhospitable shore. The Sea Transport Officer eventually sent

CATHAY blows up after disembarking troops at Bougie.
(Courtesy of Imperial War Museum - A13020)

them along to the *ODYSSEUS* in the hope that we could give them temporary shelter.

Although our accommodation was already stretched to the limit and we were, by then, very short of food with no fresh stores at all, we did the best we could for them that night. Captain Ruig sent them back to the naval control office the next day where they stood around as authority wrestled with the problem of their immediate future.

Most of them were ship's firemen of a breed well schooled to meet dilemma with calm resignation, but one became truculent as our Captain was going ashore. Our mild mannered Bo'sun who was standing near the gangway and clearly feared the worst, immediately flattened him as if it was all in the day's work. The shipmates of the unfortunate man smiled broadly at the entertainment.

Less happily they learned later they were being sent back to Algiers by rail, a journey of such extreme discomfort and uncertainty that even the worst sea journey would be preferable we were informed.

To supplement our meagre diet we bought ample quantities of dates which we found nourishing. We had also begun picking at the army rations given us for emergency use. The army's powdered, front line substitute for tea was particularly welcome, By then our own stocks were nearly out.

The enemy left us in peace as we finished discharging our war load and the laborious work of cleaning out the holds and hosing them down was undertaken with marked enthusiasm. Despite the unusual circumstances it was still a matter of pride, founded upon the soundest commercial considerations, to present them as immaculate for the next consignment.

There was an eagerness among us to get away to sea, free of the nagging thought of such a noxious cocktail under our belt. The knowledge that we would soon be loading another one was a contemplation for a later day. For the time being we enjoyed our sense of release and hoped for a speedy departure.

The auguries seemed good. Our sleep was not disturbed through the night and, when I was called to take over the watch at 4.00am, Philippeville slumbered in its peaceful setting beyond the quays whose ·shadowy stockpiles and odorous reminder provided the only evidence of belligerent engagement.

Apart from a lonely sentry, a member of the Pioneer Corps I think, no-one stirred. He could smell the coffee pot simmering in our galley and looked round cautiously before coming over to accept my offer of a refill. When I asked him where he would shelter if the siren wailed he indicated a cavern-like opening between the nearby ore bunkers. He told me it was a refuge in which he slept sometimes when he was off duty.

As the dawn approached I went forward to collect my pipe and was returning amidships when the plaintive warning sounded. With the gunner on watch I searched in the dark for the alarm button so improbably placed among a cluster of rivet heads along a bulkhead, but it was scarcely necessary as we lay barely a hundred yards from the naval control building on which the siren was mounted.

Long before its undulating tones had died away there came the first whiff of potent smoke, and all ears strained to pick up the earliest sounds of the enemy's approach. There was the metallic sound of guns being checked and· magazines lined up, and an unexplained banging from the starboard side of the wheelhouse, followed by a pained oath.

The Marine Sergeant had been nailing up a horseshoe, some trophy he had picked up ashore, and in the darkness had banged his thumb. Whatever luck it was intended to bring us, it made him our first casualty. Sucking his thumb he took charge of our defence as the distance hum of the attacking force brought us to the alert.

A voice transmitted by loud hailer from the control centre gave us a bearing on the enemy's approach. From the sound which soon filled the sky a considerable number were engaged in this change of strategy. Though it was still dark the creeping shafts of light on the eastern horizon, concealed from us by the now heavy smoke screen, must have added importantly to their overall perspective.

We heard them pass over and in anxious silence tried to assess, from the extent of that sinister throbbing, just how many consecutive attacks we would have to resist. Until the tail of the formation was overhead not a gun was fired. They were almost certainly beyond our range.

It was then that our port Oerlikon gave a defiant burst as Sergeant Bunce opened the contest. Perhaps he laid the blame for his injured thumb as the enemy's door, or it might have been his impatience to show them our mettle. His determination not to be intimidated was certainly the signal for the battle to commence.

Their leader came diving in quickly after that and suddenly all the guns in the ships and around the port were blasting away with a racket to awaken the dead. Once again we were impressed by the rate of fire from the trawler's ancient twelve-pounder whose breech must have been steaming as the shells and cordite cartridges were pushed home.

Our bridge vibrated with the pounding of our own more rapid but smaller calibre contribution, and the only sounds distinguishable above the din were the whistle of bombs and the scream of engines as one attacker quickly followed another. There seemed to be no lull but occasionally, through the tumult and the smoke, came disjointed snatches of amplified encouragement from the loud hailer at the control base.

The foul smog was at its thickest. Eyes were watering and burning and everyone was coughing, but the gunners paused only to remove their spent magazines and to snap fresh ones into place. Our counteractive senses, especially our ears, left us in no doubt that this time our attackers were really on the ball. With each successive assault along the line of the quay it became more evident that it was only a matter of time before one of them hit a jackpot.

Jack Ridler, who had been noting each wide delivery with remarkable detachment, seemed almost ready to accept the not unfamiliar theory, expressed by Jim van Ommeren, that so long as we could hear the bombs coming they were not for us. Sparks told me he was worried about his radio aerial so perilously exposed to the stream of fire. Its chances of remaining intact did seem slender.

Before being caught up in military adventures overseas *ODYSSEUS* had been equipped with two Lewis machine guns of World War One vintage, chronically subject to a wide variety of stoppages old age had not reduced. When her Oerlikon cannon had been installed, they had been stowed away as museum pieces at the back of the chartroom.

Now the bombers seemed to be pressing their attacks at a much lower height Ted Maloney, the gunner from Battersea, and I had the same thought. Their tracers might yet serve to deter. Relieved to be active we dragged them out with their pans of ammunition and carried them to the rear of the wheelhouse.

Using a high locker to give them support and to angle them away from the ship's funnel, we were too busy striving to load them in the darkness to hear the next attacker coming in. We certainly heard it begin its dive and caught some unparliamentary language from our Royal Marine. The firing around us had reached its crescendo and we did not hear it pulling out.

Before we could fire a round and with a suddenness that severed all sensation but that of intense upward pressure, the infernal orchestration stopped dead. The *ODYSSEUS* seemed to rise out of the water as the black cloud which immersed us became a crushing, irresistible force.

I can't remember the butt of that Lewis gun being wrenched from my shoulder or any impact with the deck, but when Ted and I recovered our senses we were stretched out on the opposite side of the bridge. The ship had sunk back in the water with an impact which sent a wave foaming along the quay and we felt her lurch violently to port.

By the time we had gingerly tested our arms and legs and pulled ourselves up, she began to take a heavy list to starboard.

We hurried round to that side of the bridge and were dismayed to find the two gunners there lying on the deck as if dead. But they were only stunned. One of them I knew as Butch was wounded in the arm and the other, Jim Nevarde, was holding his side.

He claimed he would soon be alright and directed our attention to another gunner lying below us on the boat deck at the foot of the bridge ladder. He seemed to be badly hurt, but was trying to get to his feet as we reached him. At that moment we heard another attacker beginning its dive and saw the Bombardier and Butch trying to re-cock their cannon.

Sparks and I had to lend them a hand heaving on the lanyard to overcome its powerful spring. At least two of our cannons were firing before the next stick of bombs was released, but there was an ominous silence from the trawler astern and we feared the worst.

This time we heard the bombs whistling and ducked as they burst along the quay. We held our breath until we realised there was to be no chain reaction from the explosive stocks we had unloaded. The fact that our ship was free of them was an agreeable bonus.

Somehow I had got the idea that she had received a direct hit on the afterdeck, but quickly concluded that the bombs had burst alongside. From snatches of conversation on the bridge and the sound of conversation via the voice pipe it was clear though that Captain Ruig was anxious about the damage below the water line. The list to port had quickly increased and it was evident that the ballast tanks were being adjusted to hold her like that.

I found the gunner we had left on the boat deck squatting on a stool outside the Captain's door. Inside the mate was busy giving first aid to the gunner from the after gun position, who was dazed and bleeding from one ear. When I helped his wounded shipmate in we discovered that he had a slice taken out of his leg and was bleeding badly and it took some time to get a satisfactory dressing on the injury.

Yet on the whole it appeared that we had so far come out of it fortunately. No one had been killed and the ship was showing no signs of settling in the water. It was getting lighter and the havoc on deck was beginning to reveal itself. There had not been another attack and quite soon the "All Clear" sounded.

The most important inspection was in the holds where the light from the early sun formed dazzling patches opposite the gaping holes we had acquired in our starboard plates. Some of the largest ones were below the level where our water line would have been had we been loaded or would be in all probability if our port list was not maintained.

The pumps had been working overtime and soon we were able to move some of the dunnage to check for any damage lower down. If the *ODYSSEUS* looked like a colander from the inside her exterior had all the appearance of some diabolical rash, awesome in its extent and even more so when we realised that one day soon, when it was repaired, we would have to repaint it.

The shambles above the main deck took longer to check, there seemed so much of it. Indeed evidence of the attack was to turn up continually as a grim reminder of the occasion well after we had come to terms with it. The immediately obvious damage had left cabins and compartments without their heavy teak doors which lay splintered about the deck, portholes without their glass, ventilators without cowls, and heavy steel derricks drilled through. Wire stays had been cut away, stanchions smashed or flattened and, though Jack Ridler's aerial seemed still intact, there was much aloft needing to be repaired or renewed.

It was whilst we were working our way through that first inspection in full daylight that someone realised that the Nederlands flag was no longer flying from our ensign staff. It was a matter of pride that it should always be there, but now it lay torn and discoloured among the debris on the poop. The second mate quickly produced a brand new one and an audience watched anxiously as I shinned up the staff to renew the halyard block. There was a cheer from the ship and from some soldiers on the quay as the colours were run up.

If breakfast was late that morning the cook could be excused. The blast had swept through the galley with devastating effect, but he complained most of a steel fragment which had cut its way through the starboard side, torn through the large metal bin in which he mixed his dough for our bread and gone out through the port side leaving a large ventilation hole in the steel plate.

George, the deck boy, had a proud memento. He had been blown through one door of the galley and out the other side. Examining himself for injuries he could only find a hole in the front of his jersey and in the shirt beneath. It was only when he examined the steel whistle which was hanging from his neck, suspended over his chest, that he found the explanation. A steel fragment had penetrated the front of the whistle and dented the back of it.

One of the naval gunners was examining the severed heel of a boot which had been stowed in his seabag. It had been neatly cut off by a bomb fragment which had carved its way through the side of their accommodation, passed through the mattress on his bunk, through his bag, and then torn its way out through the other side of the cabin to spend its force against the side of the Captain's apartment opposite.

Such revelations, and there were several others, caused me and Ted Maloney to take a closer look at the place where we crouched behind the wheelhouse to load our Lewis guns. We were not surprised to find the ventilator against which we had braced ourselves, leaning drunkenly and exhibiting a gaping hole at head height.

The *ODYSSEUS* was not the only ship to have been damaged. The *OUSEL* damaged previously had again suffered and her seaworthiness was now in question. The trawler had also taken some blast and we were sad to learn that at least one of her gun's crew had been severely wounded.

CHAPTER SIX

Soon an army ambulance arrived to pick up the wounded. It also collected the casualties from the naval trawler, including one man we were told who was not expected to survive. We watched them driven off to a nearby British field hospital, I think. Then for us the hard work began.

Getting the ship ready for sea was a problem. She was obviously in no condition to sail as she was. Only the contrived list was preserving her buoyancy. To bring her back on to an even keel would first require extensive repair work to seal the gaping holes below her water line on the now exposed starboard side.

Philippeville had no facilities for such surgical engineering and the Captain was anxious, as we all were, to get back to Algiers with the least delay. Happily, a team of Royal Navy shipwrights was found and, with an optimism which indicated much previous experience, it accepted the challenge of making us watertight for that journey at least. Even as a first-aid job it was going to take time, but they seemed confident they could make the *ODYSSEUS* seaworthy again and ready to depart with the next convoy.

It was decided we move back to a buoy in the outer harbour, but before we did so there was an illuminating interlude which further revealed our Marine Sergeant's single-minded intention to meet the enemy with any stray shaft opportunity provided.

Our stocks of 20mm ammunition were, by now, much depleted and replenishment had not been forthcoming. With an uncertain sea trip ahead of us economy in that department was obviously far from the Sergeant's mind. At some stage, whilst in Philippeville, he had acquired a wheelbarrow which had caused much amused comment when he was seen pushing it up the gangway one night.

Now he produced it and with conspiratorial urgency appealed to Jim van Ommeren and me to help him collect some important stores which he claimed were waiting for us along the quay. He did not say what they were, but I think we both guessed. The wooden ammunition boxes were stacked out of sight behind a cargo shed and they could well have been meant for us.

We managed to balance two of them in the barrow and were on our way back to the ship, the Sergeant and I steadying them as Jim pushed. Suddenly the voice of authority brought us to a halt. An

ODYSSEUS at Algiers showing a section of the riddled hull which earned her the nom de guerre - S.S. "Pepperpot". Captain Ruig stands on the quay. Ted Maloney of the Maritime Regiment keeps gangway watch.

officer in naval uniform who must have been watching our strange procession from a nearby office demanded to know what the blazes we were doing with his ammunition.

Sergeant Bunce never turned a hair. He first looked surprised, then glared at us with feigned irritation, and then made a handsome apology for having been misinformed. No-one could have doubted that he was the victim of a misunderstanding brought about by us.

It was a truly admirable performance for which we readily forgave him, even when he curtly instructed us to wheel his lost spoils back. Jim tried not to chuckle and later was to include a fair imitation of it in his repertoire of mimicry. The Sergeant was not so amused when we told him we had left his wheelbarrow behind and by that time we were moving out to the buoy.

We were soon too busy to be concerned about any shortage of ammunition. Stages had to be slung over the side as the naval shipwrights got to work. Whilst they bolted steel plates over the biggest holes and gashes, we were kept busy shaping wooden plugs which were hammered into the less spectacular openings. There were hundreds of them and by nightfall we were nowhere near the finish.

A solitary enemy plane came over that night, but in obedience to a pre-arranged agreement no-one opened fire. We listened to it circling the area and heard it fly off without attempting to attack. We slaved all the next day and the shipwrights had made so much progress above and below the water line that soon we were able to reduce her list.

They had seen a good deal of enemy inflicted damage on a wide variety of warships and merchant vessels and appeared genuinely surprised that *ODYSSEUS*, with no armour or reinforced plating, had survived the encounter. Their analysis revealed something encouraging about the old girl that I had not realised. Her plates and frame, fashioned in Germany soon after the Great War, were of wrought iron. Such outdated construction had bestowed on her much greater strength than many a steel ship could call on in critical moments.

The shipwrights also pointed out to us, among the innumerable perforations in her topsides and superstructure, many smaller holes which they claimed were caused by cannon shells. No-one aboard had been aware of any gunfire from above during the attack, but it was certainly something else to bear in mind.

The convoy we were to join later that day was signalled as we were still taking in the stages, and two were still hanging over the starboard side as we cast off from our buoy. There were still many holes unplugged, but none that would seriously endanger our buoyancy. The mate's initial report had dealt only with the damage we could easily see. Much of it above the main deck was still concealed and would be revealed only in the course of time.

Although one of our gunners had been left in hospital our numbers had not depleted. In Philippeville the chief steward had taken on an assistant, a young man from Holland who had been working there as an interior decorator until his home had been wrecked by a bomb.

He was a cheerful recruit who told us he had really gone to North Africa as an artist. It was a picturesque country. Events which had trapped him there had made it necessary for him to find a more commercial role. Now he was anxious to get to Britain and the *ODYSSEUS* had turned up at an opportune time. His optimism was not shared by all, but was welcome nevertheless, if only for its tonic effect.

Our return voyage to Algiers was not without its moments of drama, though I managed to sleep through one of them. During the

MERCANTILE MACHINE GUNNERS' COURSE

CERTIFICATE OF PROFICIENCY

No. **52500**

─ 3 JUL 1942

M. N. S. T. O.
CARDIFF

....
Date stamp of Training Centre.

Name GEORGE GLENTON.

Rating DECK DEPT. ·D.B. No. R.237208.

has completed the Mercantile Machine Gunners' Course

and has qualified as a Machine Gunner for duty in D.E.M.

Ships.

H Wadsworth.
....
D.E.M.S. Officer.

COMMANDER. R.N.R.
....
Rank.

P.T.O.

Many men of the merchant ships crews held an official licence to join in.

night the alarm bell sounded and there was a simultaneous burst of fire from one of our guns. Sergeant Bunce had spotted a torpedo and had opened up at it to indicate its direction to all ships around. It gave us a wide enough berth and was not heard of again.

When I went on watch at 4.00am Jim, who had been on look-out above the wheelhouse and was not the man to mistake the track of a curious dolphin for that of its dreaded simile, told me he had sighted another one heading straight for our bow. It had passed out of sight as he waited for the explosion, but we were sailing light and it must have passed under our stern, having been set to run too deep.

The remainder of the night and the next day were without incident. The only concern was for the gunner who had been exposed to the blast in our after gun box two nights before. He was still very dazed and was obviously suffering from severe concussion.

We arrived at Algiers in the late afternoon and went straight inside to berth alongside a British coaster which had accompanied us in the convoy from Britain. She was the *MORAY COAST*, one of Coast Lines' smart fleet of diminutive motor ships, easily recognisable in spite of her grey disguise.

Her crew informed us that they had been kept in Algiers since our first arrival and had still to discharge their cargo. The warmth inspired by our reunion cooled somewhat when we learned that she carried aviation fuel, and when the Captain heard of it we were put to work at once, passing wires across the dock in order to warp ourselves as far from her as possible in the event of an air attack.

When the siren sounded at 2.00am we, accordingly, heaved her across the basin, and back again when the anticipated raid failed to develop. The next day we moved her again, to a berth further along the quay. If our Captain intended to make us a less vulnerable target we had no complaints but Eric told me that once, in a British port, he had ordered her to be moved every day for a week.

It was his opinion that the Captain couldn't bear it if his crew were not busy. I formed a different theory when we were called out to move her again on the following day, and this time found ourselves in a berth on one of the inner quays which gave us much easier access to the social intercourse of that bustling yet mysterious city.

Full marks to Captain Ruig. At last we had a chance to find a barber and by that time most of us needed a trim. For Jim and others with a more congenial sense of priority it brought us within walking distance of a cafe or two, and a harbour bar. There was an enthusiasm among the younger element in the crew to explore further afield, but that opportunity had to be delayed whilst we applied ourselves to the more urgent work of restoring the ship to something of its former order.

It was December and less than a week to Christmas. When the mate eventually declared a free afternoon Eric, Jacob Harteveld and I headed for the Boulevard Laferriere with its shops and promenade and every evidence of a mounting festive spirit. It was clearly heightened by the recent events which had so dramatically caused the hasty departure of the Axis Armistice Commission and all its depressing effect of enemy control.

The effects of more than two years of enforced neutrality were all too obvious. Though the fashionable shops were brightly decorated the absence of imported goods showed sadly beyond the tinsel. Even the toy shops, bare of most things but ingeniously crafted wooden playthings, told the tale of lengthening deprivation. If Jacob had thoughts of what life must now be like in his motherland he tried not to show them.

We strolled to the Place du Governement with its tree lined square and picturesque mosque. It was as broad as Trafalgar Square, but almost without traffic.

What vehicles we did see were driven on gas carried in a variety of inflatable containers attached to their roofs or towed on trailers. It was a city of hills and at every gear change jets of flame streaked from their exhaust pipes.

We walked back to the ship along the Rue de la Marine, under the colonnades of La Grande Mosque. It looked ancient enough to interrupt the enjoyment of our brief freedom with thoughts of the many unfortunate European seamen of generations gone who had been brought to this great port on the Barbary Coast in saracens' chains. Somehow our voluntary term in the galleys seemed much less harsh and, we hoped, would not last nearly as long.

The distractions of the shore brought some entertaining interchange between Jim van Ommeren and the older Jacob. They were both creatures of habit, but in widely different ways. Jacob Ouwehand never went ashore without meticulous preparation. His shirt had to be spotless, his hat and suit thoroughly brushed at least twice, and his shoes highly polished. Then he had to find his tiepin and select a smart handkerchief.

It was a performance which amused Jim, particularly as he was supposed to be the untidy one and Jacob's immaculate turn out was never achieved without the fo'c'sle being left in a state of utter disorder. Jim's own wardrobe was much more modest. He had another cap, some spare dungarees and a jacket, but I don't think he owned a tie.

When he went ashore it was to some neighbourhood cafe or bar where he could meet other sailors, sometimes old shipmates, and talk shop. He was not happy away from the atmosphere of sea ports and confided in me one night on watch, that if he survived the war his one ambition was to take some longshore job in his home port of Rotterdam. It was where he had been brought up. In the meantime any other haven where sailors foregathered made a sociable substitute.

He had sailed in many ships and had experienced little else, but his general knowledge was remarkable, though I never saw him read a book. Sometimes he brought old friends aboard. He had a particular affinity with Norwegians and our cramped fo'c'sle had some merry evenings. Through his contacts we learned many things about the coastal operation we might otherwise not have known.

One thing seemed absolutely certain. Now that our seaworthiness was virtually assured following a survey and the commencement of more permanent repairs, we could expect the *ODYSSEUS* to be employed in the Mediterranean for at least as long as it took to clear the enemy from North Africa.

It was time to plan for the future and after some discussion by the 'ways and means committee' it was decided that the fo'c'sle could do with a gramophone. Financing such a purchase was a problem, but Jacob Harteveld, who was especially keen on the idea, suggested an answer.

Ever since we had been berthed on the inner quay we had been pestered by the most determined Arab traders for any spare clothes we cared to sell them. The fact that none of us except, perhaps, the older Jacob had any garment he did not need, made their persistence a nuisance. Then the younger Jacob, whilst rummaging in the forepeak locker for something or other, had discovered a large pile of abandoned clothing which must have been mouldering in that dark corner for years.

There were shabby greatcoats, old working trousers, even some well worn footwear, all items which from time to time had been flung there by successive occupants of our berths. If we had known about them before we might have given them a passage over the side on some dark night. The next time one of our local old clothes men came aboard our self-consciousness disappeared as his face lit up at the sight of our disreputable hoard.

There was no haggling. He pulled out a bulky roll of filthy 100 Franc notes and began peeling them off. Anxious not to be outbid by some later arrival he thrust a greasy wad into Jacob's hands and he and his minions whipped the pile away as if they had come into a sudden inheritance. The only snag was that we couldn't as easily find anyone to sell us a gramophone, but at least the fo'c'sle's improvement fund had been launched.

It was to be several weeks before we found one, a much-used portable, which we bought for £10 from a member of the crew of a British cargo ship on a turn-round voyage from the Clyde. The rate of exchange had by that time settled in our favour and we thought we had a bargain until we discovered its frail spring. Happily our third engineer who, like most Hollanders, had a musical inclination managed to repair it and, until we ran out of needles, it performed valiantly.

There were twelve or more records with it and we could find no others. Their aesthetic appeal ranged between George Formby's "Bullfighter" song and Edward Elgar's "Land of Hope and Glory", both of which were firm favourites with Jim who was tone deaf, but always lent his voice to them.

Four days before Christmas, acutely for me, the baneful curse on our starboard lifeboat was further confirmed. The damage it had suffered had been carefully patched up and Jacob Ouvehand and I were overhauling its gear. I was at the after end, putting my weight on the wire guy of the rotary davit, intending to make it fast, when something gave.

The momentum which threw me backwards towards the yawning edge of the unrailed boatdeck left me with only the instinct for survival. It almost saved me, but as my left hand clamped on to a lifebuoy on a bracket on the side of the radio house, my doom seemed doubly sealed. It was horse-shoe shaped and, swivelling round accompanied my downfall.

Had I not known precisely what lay under me, those seconds of anticipation as I hurtled to the after deck, a good twelve feet below, might not have been so cruel. As it was I could remember every rigid projection of the cargo winch directly in my path. Yet, as I mentally recoiled, some deep sense of preservation must have been at work. I can remember trying to hunch my back and to tuck in my legs as I fell.

The crash, when it came, was numbing, which took care of the immediate pain. The fact that I remained conscious was evidence enough that I had not been brained, but I found I could not move and was frightened I had broken my back. I recognised the mate's voice. It was an imprecation of some kind in his mother tongue.

He was quickly at my side and I was pleased to find some defensive movement in my arms as he started to pull me off my unyielding couch. Even though my back had no feeling I was conscious of its various jutting attachments and guessed I might have been impaled. The mate got the message and soon Joe Stoakes had taken over and I found myself being gently lifted away from its grim embrace.

Joyfully, by now supported on both sides, I discovered I could stand. Even in that moment of dazed surprise curiosity drew my eyes to the piece of machinery that had arrested my fall and I was vaguely astonished to see that rigid, once upright section of the stop-valve control now bent and almost horizontal.

If it had not been for the shock I was under I might easily have been overwhelmed by the general concern, but it was Jack Ridler's intervention which was soon to impress me most. The commotion which had brought him out from his quarters presented him with an immediate overall view of my plight and without delay he had set off to enlist the aid of the R.A.M.C. which had a medical aid post in the dock area.

In the meanwhile I was carefully deposited on the deck in the saloon, face down so that the mate and Joe could attend to the injury in my back. It must have looked a mess, but Joe cleaned it up and put on some kind of a dressing. The chief steward produced a tumbler of whisky, intended as an anaesthetic substitute I imagined, but I was only desperate for some water.

It wasn't wasted. The army doctor brought aboard by Jack was a Scot with an encouraging bedside manner and I noted after he had left that the whisky had also gone. After his first examination in which he made some hopefully astonished noises, he declared all my bones were intact. Then with the aid of a corporal and some clips from our medicine chest he made a professional repair to my torn flesh.

*Pre-War picture of P&O's beautiful NARKUNDA (16,632 grt),
commodore ship of the second "Torch" assault convoy. She was dive-
bombed as she left Bougie on November 14, 1942 and sank after a
further air attack. Thirty-one of her crew were killed.*
(Courtesy of P&O)

Before leaving he told me he would call back the next day and
apologised for not being able to get me into a hospital. There were
just no spare beds he claimed, but I was left with the impression he
was doing me a kindness. It was the first time the thought of being
removed ashore had crossed my mind and by that time I was feeling
sufficiently relieved not to care.

The *ODYSSEUS* had nothing resembling a sickbay. Few cargo
ships had. Our fo'c'sle with its six bunks was no ideal place for the
care and recovery of the lame and the halt, but mine was a lower berth
and I did not lack attention. After I had been deposited there, with the
mate assuming the responsibilities of hospital registrar, I felt glad
indeed that I had not been whisked ashore.

His bedside manner was a revelation in seamanlike compassion.
I was well aware how lucky I had been, but just in case I had any
doubts he confided that once he had fallen half the height of my
dramatic descent and as a result had been laid up for months with two
broken legs. I was only too willing to believe his earnest assurance
that he would have me back on duty again in no time at all.

The chief steward who had rarely been seen down forrard brought me oranges and an armful of reading material from his own carefully hoarded store. Lying on my stomach I was grateful, but in no position to have much use for either at that stage. Such titbits as he delivered were a well received addition to the fo'c'sle fare and balm to my conscience, knowing that being one man short on deck was no bonus for them.

We were now very much of a family and no-one ever mentioned that. Their attentions were encouraging and practical and had much to do with my ready acceptance of a situation which was at times painfully frustrating. There was another reason why I was glad to be still with them.

My readiness to join the crew at the last minute was not without self-interest. I had been keen then not to waste any unnecessary time ashore because of the accumulation of sea service I still needed as a minimal qualification for the humblest watchkeeping certificate.

It pleased me to think that however long I languished in that bunk it would still be mounting up.

My mind was also occupied with the esoteric attraction that had drawn me to *ODYSSEUS*. Homer could be blamed for that and though I could have wished for a translation of his "Odyssey" it was in my mind that somewhere beyond the Tunisian border lay the land of the Lotus Eaters from which Odysseus had reclaimed his crew on their tortuous homeward voyage from Troy.

The thought had struck me on our recent east bound voyage that soon, if the First Army's campaign succeeded, our battle scarred *ODYSSEUS* might yet get that far. Lying on my belly and wondering about the future it somehow seemed an attractive and wholly satisfying ambition.

CHAPTER SEVEN

My uncomfortable confinement became less irksome as the days passed. Eric quickly proved how competent he might otherwise have been as a male nurse and showed an encouraging determination to have me walking again as soon as possible. It also brought me into closer relationship with other members of the crew who up till then had, by virtue of our different duties, been nodding acquaintances.

Their obvious concern was comforting evidence of the tight bond which our shared dangers had woven for us. There was curiosity too, and I was to be reminded of my good fortune when my visitors handled the broad bladed knife in its leather sheath which had deflected the protruding control on the winch from my possible impalement.

To take my mind off my own problems I became concerned about the health of George, the deck boy, whose condition had deteriorated since the blast had flung him across the deck at Philippeville. He had made no complaint to anyone aboard and certainly seen no doctor.

When the R.A.M.C. doctor made his daily visit to check my condition he readily agreed to examine him and quickly arranged for George to be taken ashore. He must have been in a serious way. It was the last any of us saw of him.

Christmas Eve began like any other day with so little flavour of customary good cheer that Scrooge might well have approved. There were plenty of personal reasons, not counting the breakfast, for members of the crew to view the occasion with some melancholy and even irony.

It was Jim who took the necessary steps to restore something of the festive spirit we had sensed ashore as Christmas approached. In his mysterious way he had acquired a bottle of whisky from the store we had long been aware the Captain guarded jealously.

When the doctor came aboard with his orderly to make his morning examination of my condition, the glasses quickly appeared and soon the fo'c'sle rang with the cheerful talk of voluntary exiles happy enough to let the spirit flow and to make the best of it. Before taking his leave the Scots medic, specifically referring to my health, said he now considered me out of danger.

During the afternoon a drama which had little enough to do with Christmas was unfolding on the shore. One of the gunners on watch at the gangway first became aware of it, but it was some time before the details were brought aboard. Admiral Darlan, Former French naval chief and Vichy Government cabinet minister, who had been in Algiers when the Allies landed and had agreed to join their cause, had been assassinated.

He had been shot dead by a French student who bluffed his way into the Admiral's office and emptied a pistol into him. He was undoubtedly the victim of political intrigue and his death brought a cloud of suspicion to darken the occasion.

Whatever headaches his murder caused the Allied commanders in their offices ashore were pure speculation to those aboard ship. No doubt there was considerable concern over the Admiral's replacement as Governor General and much distraction organising his state funeral. His killer was tried and executed within a few days of the event.

The next day our main concern was to contemplate how well the ship's cook would rise to the challenge of our Christmas dinner. It also brought us the chance to observe our dour Captain in party mood, a performance I had no intention of missing. It was the first day I attempted to walk more than a few steps and with the help of Eric Adams managed, after a few false starts, to negotiate the foredeck and the ladder amidships, an obstacle course at the best of times.

The saloon was crowded and apart from the crew, including the gunners, there were several guests from the shore. Captain Ruig arrived from his quarters above using his own companionway, beaming in the manner of a star performer about to give his best to a role demanded of him by the occasion.

As he supervised the measuring out of the drinks from an array of bottles, Jim van Ommeren observed in a voice drowned by the hubbub: "If he had dressed up as Father Christmas we would really have had to worry." Nevertheless the festive atmosphere soon took over and the guests, friends of the Captain, clearly enjoyed themselves, Scotch whisky having been so long a rarity on shore.

There were presents too. At one stage in the proceedings the Captain indicated a number of cardboard cartons and instructed the third mate to hand them round to those whose names they bore. As there were not sufficient to go round some had to be shared between two or three members of the ship's company.

They contained tins of cigarettes, woollen scarves, chocolate bars and biscuits and some jars of honey. Each box contained some pen and ink sketches made by school children in the Dutch East Indies, now occupied by the Japanese invaders. Jim, who had sailed to those parts and had no illusions as to how the young artists might have fared subsequently, was especially moved.

The party came to an end when the Captain made a brief speech which owed its success to the cockney interjections of the army gunner, Ted Maloney, whose customary wit transformed it into a crosstalk act. If the Captain was less than amused he earned full marks for not showing it.

The cook earned some good marks also. By some means, known only to the chief steward, some Berber farmer had been persuaded to part with enough chickens to mark the occasion and the galley roasted them to near perfection. From our rapidly decreasing stores the steward produced some rare cans of pineapple and on such regal fare we could acknowledge it was Christmas at last.

The real entertainment came after dark. The alarm bell sounded as I was getting off to sleep and I realised, I think for the first time, the handicap I now suffered and was glad that I had given my legs a preliminary try out. I could hear some distant gunfire and I assumed it was from the auxiliary anti-aircraft ship the *ALYNBANK* which for a long period had been stationed in the Bay as a first line of defence.

Her longer range radar system had for long provided early warning of approaching planes for the port and the sound of her eight four-inch guns and other weapons had been the prelude to previous attacks we had experienced at Algiers. Quickly her fire was joined by the guns of other ships and from batteries ashore.

There was the sound of planes making their attacks and noise of gunfire reaching its crescendo from all round. Lying there I tried to identify from the din how many planes were involved, but found it impossible. Suddenly between spasms of gunfire I heard the sound of accordion music and realised that, in some ship not too far away, spirited souls were not allowing the intrusion of the enemy to spoil their Christmas entertainment.

Eventually I heard one plane diving in for its bombing run with engines at full pitch, but instead of them eventually fading away as it pulled out, the sound rose to a scream and abruptly ceased. It seemed that one enemy airman at least would not be seeing in the New Year.

70

Soon the gunfire died away and the sound of music and voices singing took over as various celebrations, amplified across the waters of the Bay, found a new lease of life.

Though it was easy to detect the somewhat forced and vaguely desperate holiday feeling in the atmosphere, Algiers was no bed of roses far behind the lines.

Reports brought back by the crew from their forays ashore indicated a firm resentment in some sections of the French population to the Allied presence. Those who had arrived there via Marseilles to escape conditions in France could not have been too pleased about the frequent bombing raids it had brought in its train, apart from the disruption in the city caused by the establishment of the various military and political headquarters by the British and Americans.

There was certainly frustration among the shopkeepers who might have welcomed such an injection of new customers if only they had had anything to sell. To see so many ships arriving from overseas, laden with every sort of war supply, mostly to be tran-shipped down the coast, with only the faintest hope of any crumbs falling their way must also have caused some resentment.

In spite of the many thousands of tons of cargo unloaded in the port since the first troops had landed, there still seemed to be shortages of many of the supplies which would have made life easier for those servicemen who laboured mightily to keep that maritime conveyor belt going.

The delayed arrival of an R.A.F. radar warning system, the belated delivery of materials to make emergency airfields operational in the wet weather, were the hazards only to be expected of so bold an operation launched from so long and dangerous a distance. But there were numerous other shortages which only time could take care of.

At the medical post along the quay, where I went soon after Christmas to have the clips removed from my injured back, I discovered the army medics had no clip extractors. It led to an amusing confrontation with the mate when I returned to the ship to rummage through our medical chest. He had no idea what they looked like either.

As chief officer, responsible for all the gear aboard, apart from the chief steward's and engine room stores, he was reluctant to allow any of our basic collection of surgical instruments out of his sight. The battle between his natural compassion and stern duty was a diversion I much enjoyed, especially when he jumped at my suggestion that he should return to the army post with me to keep an eye on his charges.

The orderly who quickly identified the instrument, so rudimentary as to have escaped our attention, might well have wanted to keep it. Whilst he was redressing my back he told me that they were so short of medical supplies they were under orders to use the same dressing materials again and even to use the same plaster strips twice whenever it was possible.

A couple of days later when the Scots medical officer saw my wound was showing early signs of infection, he looked considerably annoyed and quickly went ashore. He was soon back with a glass phial containing no more than a spoonful of white powder. It was sulphanilamide, a recently developed anti-bacterium he told me, and added "That's the last we have. God knows when we will get any more!"

The shipwrights had in no way been idle over Christmas and were getting on well with the extensive repairs to our plates, but we were still in their hands when the New Year arrived. Within a few hours of it being welcomed in, the *ODYSSEUS* got an unexpected addition to her casualty list. To celebrate the departure of 1942 the steward had provided the fo'c'sle with some bottles of local wine, a rare enough treat, which undoubtedly had something to do with it.

The Bo'sun in an unusually progressive mood took it upon himself, as a New Year's resolution, to persuade the cook to upgrade his performance in 1943. That gentleman, faced with the largest and most powerful member of the crew, justifiably retreated across the galley without pausing to identify which of his alleged culinary sins he was to answer for. The Bo'sun went after him, slipped on a greasy patch of deck and crashed into the cast iron stove.

The cook, further alarmed by the anticipation of the wrath to come through this added cause of dissatisfaction, made his escape. The Bo'sun got to his feet, with one wing hanging limply, waved aside all offers of assistance with his good arm and strode off in search of a restorative.

Eventually he allowed the mate to put his arm in a sling and was conveyed to hospital for professional attention, but only under protest. It was of small consolation to him to learn later that the crew's meals improved immediately, though our hard pressed and much maligned cook had by that time abandoned his post and fled ashore.

Things only got back to normal two days later when Captain Ruig sternly intervened and ordered the chastened despot of the galley back to his post. The Bo'sun who suffered little more than a dislocation returned later, having been kept in for observation. He claimed he had enjoyed his rest and smiled broadly when the assistant cook told him, with feigned solemnity, that the Captain was going to charge him the cost of repairing the cracked galley stove.

Perhaps the most disappointed man was the Sergeant of Marines whose own vendetta with the cook rumbled on. Yet he had other things on his mind as he visibly chafed at our necessary delay in port. He had acquired a replenishment of our ammunition and was anxious to put some more of it to use in the furtherance of some newly evolved theory of his own as to how torpedo planes should best be dealt with.

The New Year was heralded with a spectacular display of gunfire which did not last long and was generously ascribed to a false alarm. A few days later, with our repairs completed, we moved to a loading berth.

It was not accomplished without some drama and some further damage, due entirely to the over enthusiasm of the local dock pilot eager to vaunt his skill. In that crowded harbour it was a difficult approach with a French ship lying off the quay, along which we were to berth, and a large British ship with a high counter stern lying alongside. Passing smartly between the two the pilot stopped our engines, but narrowly miscalculated in swinging our stern towards the empty berth.

With so little space to play with and no time to spare there was not much he could do to gain those extra feet of clearance or to check her swing. It was a disaster in slow motion as the stern of the *ODYSSEUS* moved inexorably under the counter of the larger ship. The mouths of the soldiers on the quay, waiting to load us, dropped open as of one accord. The eyes of those of us on the poop became riveted to the looming steel plates and the closing gap.

There was a deathly silence and suddenly it became all too evident that we were going to collide. The hush was broken by the cry of the second mate calling upon me to get a fender - an order he was never allowed to forget - but by that time I was heading for the after deck with Joe Stokes and Jim. Before the grinding crunch came the second mate had joined us, fascinated spectators to that clash of steel.

We had expected the after gun box and the two tall ventilators to be swept away, but fortunately the other ship was almost unloaded and the upward sweep of her old fashioned stern saved us from severe damage.

Our poop looked a sorry sight nevertheless with the stanchions of its starboard rail snapped off or bent flat, and the heavy ventilator on that side leaning at a dangerous angle. There were some nasty dents along our counter and much paintwork in need of restoration. Captain Ruig, who had been glaring aft in grim silence as the pilot's error approached its climax, left him in no doubt of our corporate feelings once the ship was securely berthed.

The quay was piled high with all manner of dangerous cargo waiting transhipment, but we were relieved to see a consignment of steel runway sections and bags of cement obviously intended as part of our load. We greeted such a solid contribution to the improvement of air cover further along the coast as a double bonus for the New Year.

We were soon loaded by as cheerful a unit of army dockers as we had yet met, men existing on basic rations and still living under the greatest discomfort who were determined not to let it get them down. Their song and patter as they laboured, much of which might have won applause from a music hall audience, kept us entertained.

When Jim van Ommeren, who felt a deep sympathy for all men in uniform, suggested they could be well employed on tour their Sergeant, himself a man of no mean wit, said: "Not bloody likely. When the lads get these hatchboards off in Philippeville they won't be laughing. They're expecting a consignment of beer!"

The next morning, soon after dawn, we moved out to the mole to await the next eastbound convoy, mooring stern on close to a British cargo ship which had been damaged by a torpedo. She was the *HARMATTAN*, belonging to the London firm of J. & C. Harrison, and had been torpedoed just off Algiers in December. Another British ship, the *OCEAN VANQUISHER*, had been hit at the same time. Both were severely damaged and lying in Algiers out of action.

On the day they were attacked a third vessel, the *EMPIRE CENTAUR*, had fallen victim whilst lying in the Bay to a more sinister style of assault, peculiar to the courageous ingenuity of a diabolical branch of the Italian Navy. A dozen or more frogmen operating from a submarine had evaded the defence patrols and some of them had succeeded in attaching a limpet mine to the underside of her hull.

The P&O Liner STRATHALLAN (23,722 grt) - fifth and largest of the company's North African losses was torpedoed by U-562 north of Oran. Nearly all her 5,000 troops and a contingent of nurses were rescued, but an attempt to tow her into port failed when she capsized and sank on December 22, 1942.

(Courtesy of P&O)

All the frogmen had been captured, we were told, but the ship was now also out of action as a result of the delayed explosion. It was a repeat of the even more successful raid at Alexandria the year before in which the British battleships, *VALIANT* and *QUEEN ELIZABETH*, and other vessels had been severely damaged. At that time it had also been used with serious effect in the anchorage off Gibraltar and had resulted in some cargo ships being sunk by mysterious explosions whilst in convoy.

The Christmas and the New Year period had not been kind to Allied shipping in North Africa. The loss of another P&O liner, the much admired *STRATHALLAN*, as she approached Oran carrying over 4,000 troops and a detachment of Queen Alexandra nurses was a severe blow. Fortunately, though lives were lost in the engine room when a U-boat torpedo struck her, all the passengers and the remainder of the crew were rescued before she sank, just a few miles from that port, after attempts to tow her in.

From our various sources of information ashore we gathered that the mounting losses in ships sunk or badly damaged at sea and port was causing alarm among those in charge of the vast supply operation. Rumour had it that more than twenty ships had succumbed to the enemy's persistent attacks in less than a fortnight and, without doubt, the ports to the east, especially Bone, had suffered worst.

In the early hours of the New Year that vital harbour had been attacked with full fury from the air and two cargo ships, the *NOVEL-IST* owned by T. & J. Harrison of Liverpool, and the *HARPALYCE* belonging to J. & C. Harrison of London, had sustained much damage. On the following day the South American Saint Line's ship *ST MERRIEL* and British Tankers' *EMPIRE METAL* were sunk with heavy loss of life. Other ships had been badly damaged and the port installations had taken such a beating that ships were now having to use their own lifting gear to discharge.

We heard also of the loss at sea of the fine new cargo liner *BENALBANACH*, some 150 miles to the north-east of Algiers whilst on route to Bone. She carried 400 troops and was heavily laden with explosives, petrol, motor vehicles and tanks when she was hit by two aerial torpedoes. She was set on fire following explosions and sank within two minutes. There were only forty survivors.

The men of the royal Engineers dock units were unusually glum when the news was passed on for she had been one of the ships aboard which some of them had trained for their present operation. It had happened only a few days before and about the same time and on the same route the Messageries Maritime steamer *VILLE DE STRASBOURG*, now in Allied service, had also been torpedoed by a U-boat, but had made it to port.

The stricken STRATHALLAN, heavily on fire, loses her fight for survival a few miles from Oran.
(Courtesy of P&O)

Such tidings made it abundantly clear the enemy was, if anything, stepping up its determined offensive to break or severely disrupt the Allies' extended and still dangerously exposed supply line with all the forces they could muster.

Under such circumstances it seemed only logical that, in order to limit the scale of loss, those in charge of our destiny would extend their dependence on the fleet of smaller ships under their control. Under the conditions prevailing the transhipment of more cargoes at Algiers and Oran seemed eminently sensible.

Jim was in the mate's black book. He had met some old shipmates from Rotterdam and gone adrift for a couple of nights. When he returned he confided in Eric and me that he had been offered a berth aboard their ship, but Captain Ruig had put his foot down. He was philosophical about it and chose to see it as a triumph of sorts - proof that, even to Amsterdam sailors, a Rotterdam man was indispensable.

The assistant steward we had left behind on our previous trip rejoined us even though his berth had now been filled. He was given the job of doing the laundering and found a spare berth in the firemen's quarters. The greaser we had abandoned had gone to another ship and one of the firemen had got his job. As a replacement a remarkably versatile Arab was recruited.

Not only did he speak Dutch, French and German and several other languages, but he was a very good fireman able to keep up our head of steam without apparent effort. He had worked his passage from Marseilles in a tug after being imprisoned for a time by the German occupation force in France. His tales of occupied Europe became a fascinating diversion and brought some suspicion that he was an enemy agent which made him laugh.

We also welcomed aboard two new gunners to replace the two we had lost who were both now aboard the damaged *SCYTHIA* still waiting to sail for home. They were D.E.M.S. ratings. One was a Scot, James Johnston, from Stirling and the other, Dave Bowdley, hailed from Wolverhampton.

They were a cheerful pair and quickly made themselves at home, neither being under any illusion about our future employment. Dave had spent some time in convoy service to North Russia and had the interesting theory that many of the German flyers now engaged against us along the North African coast had been switched from their bases nearer the Arctic Circle. He claimed to recognise their tactics.

Algiers had been fairly peaceful in those early days of 1943 and, although the port was raided again the night before we sailed, we were reluctant to leave its comparative security when we were called one morning before 5.00am to take *ODYSSEUS* back to Philippeville.

CHAPTER EIGHT

It was good to feel the *ODYSSEUS* back in her element and to hear the steady heart beat of her triple-expansion engine, a gleaming mechanism whose polished movement so brightly reflected the pride of her devoted attendants. Such meticulous care was indication also of the concern her engineers must have felt at being removed by circumstances from any easily available repair facilities.

The engine room was no place for the fainthearted in such dangerous waters, but the engineers, greasers and stokehold hands were stoical beings by tradition. On the occasions when those members of the deck crew went down there to beg a pailful of hot water or to ask for steam for some appliance on deck, it was only polite to linger. There was an understandable curiosity among those below to know how the situation looked from above.

As it turned out our second trip down the coast was perhaps the most peaceful we would make during that campaign. For some reason the enemy left us with only the anticipation of their presence and we reached Philippeville soon after breakfast the following day. To our surprise we went alongside immediately to unload. There were no longer any piles of cargo on the quays and it was clear the army dockers had overhauled the backlog.

They had also got themselves a canteen of sorts and were very disappointed to learn that we had not brought their expected consignment of canned beer. When it was revealed what our main cargo was the ship was handed over to a gang of local dockers, mainly Arabs, who were now being employed to speed the work along when critical cargoes were not involved.

They made a poor second best, spending much time in lengthy argument, with the winchman frequently taking his hands off the controls to remonstrate with the ganger in screaming sessions incomprehensible to all but those involved. It was not long before a heavy stack of airfield runway plates suspended over the quay had been dropped, at the run, on the man in the truck into which they were being loaded.

All work ceased as the injured victim was extricated and removed to hospital. There was some kind of a union meeting after that and we rather hoped there would be a walk-out, but after much shouting they returned to work and the crew kept out of the way. We had other things to attend to in any case. On the way down someone had hit on the brilliant idea of replacing our damaged port liferafts with those of the half-submerged *AURORA*.

The army doctor in Algiers had told the mate to keep me on light duties, which had baffled our chief officer until I suggested painting as coming under that category, as did taking the helm and standing lookout at sea. The exercise had proved beneficial and, as cannibalising our unfortunate sister ship was a job for all hands, I was happy to take part.

It was warm under a clear sky and with no interference from the enemy we worked through the weekend dismantling both sets of wooden rafts, scraping and repainting unpunctured buoyancy drums and reassembling the framework to provide two sound liferafts for any future contingency. We also acquired a dinghy from among the litter of abandoned equipment which constituted the flotsam in that battered port.

Unhappily one of our gunners left it carelessly unattended to be appropriated quickly by the crew of another ship who no doubt admired its new paint and our repair work. Less disappointing were the results of social visits made by crew members aboard British and American cargo ships on turn-round voyages from Atlantic ports. Their practical sympathy for our prolonged stay in North Africa produced eggs and other items of food which easily made up for our lost boat.

The second mate of a smart new British ship, a former shipmate of mine, was particularly helpful and provided some favourite tobacco. He had worked his way up through the fo'c'sle, a process I was anxious to emulate, and we had much to talk about, but he passed on the sad news that our previous ship now lay on the bed of the North Sea having been sunk by bombs in Tees Bay. It was as well to be reminded of the war going on nearer home.

The Captain had been busy also in the few days we lay alongside. From a naval supply depot he was able to equip all the deck officers with blue battledress and did not forget the crew. He had arranged for those of us who needed new footwear to be supplied with boots.

At sixteen shillings a pair they might have been considered a bargain, but such consideration was not met with any undue flood of gratitude except by Jim who had in mind their barter value. Consequently, following their issue our decks did not instantly ring to the tramp of well shod feet. The boots were put aside to await the first good opportunity of exchanging them for more urgently needed requirements.

No feelings were hurt, except perhaps those of the Royal Marine Sergeant who quickly offered to demonstrate how they could be brought to a regulation shine. It was churlishly declined. The gunners who were generally more suitably equipped and still had occasional access to a Pusser's store looked on with some amusement.

The bootsman (with broad smile and cigarette) and both deck watches.
Eric Adams is to his left and Joe Stoakes to the right with Jim van Ommeren
on the outside. Jaapy Ouwehand stands in front, with the author and
Jacob Harteveld in the background.

Only four days after arriving our holds were clear and in the darkness before the dawn we left in the company of a few other ships to join a convoy returning from Bone bound for Algiers and Oran. We had barely got under way before the alarm sounded. Within a few minutes the enemy was overhead and attracting our fire. It was a clear night with a starry sky, but it was difficult to judge how closely we were being targeted until one plane dived in our direction.

We ceased firing after a minute or two as the attackers made off. Suddenly from a distance of probably two miles there was a display of tracers and the sound of gunfire indicating that they had found their main quarry. It was the convoy we were due to join.

The battle lasted for a considerable time and, as we approached, the firing intensified. The planes circled round us constantly but only attacked us occasionally. It was like playing in the outfield and our eyes grew strained and our ears confounded, but not so the Sergeant who blazed away every now and then fully confident in his own sensory perception. As the first streaks of daylight began to stipple the sea astern the action petered out.

We kept a wary watch for any torpedo planes as the sun rose to throw our outline into dangerous relief, but the morning haze concealed no low flying menace and soon we were taking up our allotted place at the stern of the convoy. As far as we could make out there were no casualties. In other ways it was to be an eventful trip.

It was a brilliant day with wide visibility and the planes did not return. In the early afternoon when I was on lookout on the monkey island, scanning the horizon through binoculars, I heard the commodore ship signalling with her siren for an alteration of course to starboard. As I swung round to see what danger to port had caused the emergency, the sound of depth charges exploding thudded against our plates.

A few seconds later a periscope appeared not many cable lengths on our beam. As I shouted a warning the submarine's conning tower broke the surface, its bow emerged and in moments the full length of its gleaming casing was revealed.

The second mate who had only just joined me to check our new course on the standard compass goggled with his mouth wide open and I am sure my jaw had also dropped. I assumed that she had been forced into the open by the depth charges, but my main thought was that though, as she lay, we were in no instant danger from her torpedoes she could quickly have swung her bow or stern tubes towards us.

If her crew had it in mind to make some desperate bid to fulfil her interrupted mission before she was overwhelmed she could have had a field day. There was also the not insignificant gun on her foredeck which, at point blank range, could well have inflicted considerable damage if her Commander had a defiant end in mind.

For Sergeant Bunce it was a red letter day, something that could only have occurred to him in a wild dream, marred only by the fact that he had nothing larger at his command than a 20mm cannon.

The waters of the Mediterranean were still sluicing from the submarine's casing and drainage ports as we watched his shells feathering the water and ricocheting off the plates around the conning tower, from which none of her crew had yet emerged.

By this time our after gun had joined in and as the two streams of tracers converged there came the resounding crack of a twelve-pounder gun fired by a Dutch ship slightly ahead of us to port. It was well ranged and we saw the spout of water alongside as the shot arrived.

Her next round was a direct hit I think, but it had become a confused picture as other ships of the convoy joined in with weapons of various calibre, some from the inner ranks taking advantage of the narrowest angles between ships to claim a field of fire. With such depressed trajectory it seemed only a matter of time before the outlying ships began collecting some of the damage intended for the enemy.

We could see a destroyer speeding in and quickly there came the signal for a general cease fire. The convoy was moving ahead and the fate of the submarine was momentarily concealed, then suddenly we saw her bows rise as she slipped under stern first. In the glare of the sun on the water I thought I saw some kind of inflatable raft on the surface and we could see the escort ship circling the area, hopefully picking up survivors. It seemed, for any who had not escaped, a cruel way to die.

Having only once got a detailed look at a German U-boat I had thought for some reason, perhaps the shape of her conning tower and the profile of her guard rails amidships, that she was Italian. Long afterwards I came across the recorded loss of that navy's submarine *TRITONE* on that day and it may well have been her.

The scene of our encounter was in the vicinity of Bougie which had by now become a familiar danger area for daylight attack, but no stretch of that coastline could be considered anything but hostile and the setting sun found us, if anything, even more alert. But the fading light brought no attack. It came in the morning watch not long before the dawn as we approached Algiers.

Again I was on lookout above the bridge keenly scanning the water for the slightest evidence of periscope or torpedo trails, but mainly relying on my ears for the faintest sounds from the sky. The gunner on the poop and I gave the alarm together as we picked up the first murmur.

It seemed to be a single aircraft, but when nothing developed we reckoned it was one of ours and wished it had given some recognition signal to allay our fears. Our presumption was at fault and was appropriately rewarded when, a few minutes later, the ominous sound of more planes disturbed the starlit peace. Moments later the outlying escort ships were in action and soon we were all engaged in a fearful contest in which everyone of our unseen assailants seemed to be diving towards that phosphorescent gleam created by our own wake.

With sound our only guide our guns were constantly firing and the Marine Sergeant, who I had discovered was deaf in one ear, was constantly cocking his good one and giving directional orders which were frequently drowned by the barrage. He had some time before rearranged the safety barriers which limited the field of fire of the bridge Oerlikons. Now that each could fire at an angle converging only a few feet above the monkey island I was happy to leave the third mate, our gunnery control officer, crouching behind the binnacle and establish a Lewis Gun nest, with the younger Jacob as a partner, on the boatdeck.

I cannot remember whether either of us fired many rounds. We certainly never emptied the magazines of the ancient weapons whose spring tensions never seemed to be right in spite of frequent adjustments. The Bo'sun, on the other hand, who was now fully back in form and had managed to get control of the twin Marlins, blazed away fiercely only stopping to reload. He seemed impatient to keep up with the Oerlikon gunners whose discharged shell cases were soon making a brassy clatter on the steel decks.

In spite of the intensity of the gunfire the planes pressed home their attack and must have dropped many bombs on targets not easily perceived. As they withdrew we concluded that the darkness had been much on our side and that the fish had probably got the worst of it. But we were not the only objects of attack that night for later we could see streams of tracers over towards Algiers and realised that our friends there were getting an early call.

As dawn broke we could see smoke over the city, but realised it was the smoke screen dispersing. In the light of day it seemed the only damage we had suffered was to our funnel, a noble smokestack of impressive proportions whose casing was now exhibiting more holes than it previously displayed. Both Sergeant Bunce and the Bo'sun denied responsibility, but the argument continued for sometime and only broke off when we came to anchor in Algiers Bay and went to breakfast, which Jim was quick to categorise as another example of self-inflicted violation.

In the early afternoon we joined another convoy and continued our voyage to Oran to collect our next cargo. It was a port we were all looking forward to visiting, not least because of its distance to the west. Its visits from the Luftwaffe and Regia Aeronautica were apparently less frequent and its nights comparatively undisturbed.

Its approaches had a less favourable reputation owing to the frequency of submarine attacks, particularly upon those heavily laden ships on the last stage from Gibraltar after long ocean voyages. As it transpired that was not the menace we were to meet as we covered the next 180 miles or so at the modest speed dictated by the slowest vessels in our company.·

The daylight hours passed uneventfully and dusk came and went with no unhappy disturbance. It was at 9.30pm, when the concealment of the night might have generously saved us from detection, that the alarm bells sounded. The noise of many planes in our vicinity came quite suddenly as if they were pouncing from some great altitude and immediately the ships of the convoy opened up.

I was on the monkey island again and instinctively crouched down behind the binnacle as the blast of fire from our starboard gun reminded me of my danger. The third mate, who climbed up to join me, huddled beside me and suddenly remembered he had forgotten his splinter helmet. Such an opportunity of escape was not lost and I quickly offered to get it for him.

When I returned with it he had decided that the cramped platform above the wheelhouse was no place for two and as he was the gunnery control officer I was glad to leave him to it. There seemed no point in both of us getting shot by our own side. The enthusiasm of Sergeant Bunce was an admirable quality as long as one did not get in its way.

The enemy was showing an enthusiasm to match it and for once their direct attacks brought to the ear a much more precise indication of their approach. There seemed some distinct pattern in their assault as if the convoy had been divided into sections for their attention. As our particular assailants roared in to unload their bombs, the streams of tracer shells from our own guns and from those ships around us changed direction together.

At times it seemed the whole convoy was firing at the same moment and from so many directions that the sky had all the appearance of a giant shipyard with hundreds of welders streaming their sparks along every arc in the celestial sphere. There was little time for admiring the effect. Magazines needed loading and dark figures squatted about the decks as ammunition cases were opened, shells greased and passed down the chain to the man slotting them into place.

It was whilst I was engaged in this that a plane pulled out of her dive low down on the starboard quarter and I flung myself flat as the Sergeant of Marines, who must have somehow also lowered his gun's trajectory, fired a burst over the deck.

It was a lightning reaction on my part, but from my previous experience I realised in the instant I heard the plane's engines in which direction the real danger lay. If anyone had been standing in the Sergeant's field of fire his chances of survival would have been slim. In a rare lull in the proceedings I asked him if he had realised how near he had come to scoring an own goal and he sounded genuinely surprised.

Unabashed, as if such a sacrifice would have been no more than regrettable, he quickly resumed the important business in hand. The ammunition party retreated behind the shelter of the wheelhouse. Another plane was coming in low and it seemed that it had something for us. The good Sergeant was giving it all he had got as it released its bombs.

The sea astern suddenly became a fountain and a small Norwegian ship, the *MARGA* I think, rolled over until we thought she might capsize. Then we lost sight of her as the smoke from a float launched from the stern of a ship ahead drifted back and blotted out the scene. The last we saw of the Norwegian was its see-saw recovery and we hoped they had got no more than a soaking and some broken crockery.

The attack slackened off after that and I found the Sergeant pencilling notes on a piece of packing from an ammunition case. "What time did it start?" he asked and when I told him I could vaguely make out him sucking his pencil before he fired his next round. "How many direct attacks have we had?"

I had lost count, no doubt choosing through some obscure protective process of the mind to ignore some of them, but I made a guess. Sergeant Bunce then canvassed all those on the bridge and round about for any eye witness's account of anything he had hit.

There was a longish silence, then through the reeking gloom I heard him dictating to himself as he slowly wrote out his final entry: "All attacks repulsed. Planes driven off."

It was somewhat premature. The sound of the last of the departing bombers was fading away, but was soon replaced by a less distinct engine sound and renewed bursts of gunfire from distant outskirts of the convoy. Listening intently we detected aircraft low over the water, hugging the sea in fact, and almost certainly torpedo planes taking over the shift.

The gunfire was not so intense, for at such a level the flanks and outer ranks of the convoy formed a defensive barrier between the attackers and the combined fire power of the ships within. Any temptation to blaze away blindly from inside the fringes would have been a bonus indeed for any raiders who might lure the defenders to fire on themselves.

The *ODYSSEUS* was one of those ships with a clear field of fire and her guns were soon in action again, but spasmodically now as we got a rare glimpse of an assailant, or were deafened by its close approach. Most eyes were on the water following such encounters, straining to spot any torpedo tracks.

One of the gunners said he had been aware of torpedo planes earlier and believed they had scored one success, but it was difficult by sight or sound to confirm any losses by either side in such a formation at night. When the last of our latest attackers disappeared the silence seemed overwhelming, but it induced no sleep.

The Captain, I noticed, seemed particularly withdrawn and remained on the bridge. Reloading magazines and clearing up the hundreds of brass cases kept others busy and those with no immediate duty stood for a long time in groups amidships discussing in low voices the possibility of a further attack. Now that the enemy knew where to find us it seemed a strong likelihood, but the consensus was that it would come nearer the dawn.

The Sergeant was not a man to sleep when any chance of further action persisted and seemed still anxious to test opinions on how well we had done. The fact that the *ODYSSEUS* was still in her proper station and still very much afloat was a sufficiently satisfactory conclusion for most of the ship's company, but he was a professional with other things on his mind.

I had noticed that his boot laces were undone and drew it to his attention. In the darkness I could feel the revelational store welling up within him. "It's something they learned at Jutland", our veteran confided. "If you end up in the drink you'll need to kick your boots off in a hurry!" I think he was glad I had asked and by that time I was trapped.

Intrigued by his effort to log the details of the night's action I asked him if he kept a record of all such incidents, imagining that it had something to do with his anxiety to maintain our ammunition stock at a generous level. In a throaty whisper he confided in me that he was compiling a report on the best methods of defeating torpedo attacks from the air. He was writing a paper on the subject, he claimed, but whether it was by request or on his own initiative was not revealed.

The sunrise came without any further alarm and in the morning light it was possible to see that the convoy seemed very much intact with the Norwegian ship still in her position astern. It revealed also a number of the crew asleep on makeshift beds in odd corners of the boatdeck. The Bo'sun was hovering near the Marlin guns and I suspected he had not been far away from them in the past hours.

It was afternoon before we came up on Oran, easily identified by the fortress on the high westerly cape. The city itself basked peacefully, sparkling in the sunshine as we steamed into the bay. The transformation of its port area into a hive of industry, transported piecemeal across the Atlantic in many shiploads, was at first hidden from us by the sweeping mole. Suddenly we were relaxed again. Our aspirations were not high and such tranquillity promised a good night's sleep.

CHAPTER NINE

The entrance to the port was dotted with wreck buoys and the masts and upperworks of several ships, mostly sunk during the Allied landings. I was at the wheel as we went in and the French pilot told me that several of them were naval vessels scuttled by their crews before Admiral Darlan had ordered the cease fire.

One sunken vessel was so near the entrance it might easily have blocked it, but the channel was clear for ships of considerable draught. We skirted past a scuttled floating dock on which divers were working and, as Gibraltar was the nearest Allied port with such a facility, bringing it back into service was of urgent necessity.

The pilot, who had every reason to welcome the vast increase in maritime traffic, was a fund of information. The port could be very dusty he said, with winds blowing strongly from the south, and it was a season when sudden gales could turn into storms which lasted several days. Oran got air raids occasionally and he said there had been one the night before, but his account of it made it sound a very tame affair.

Once inside the mole we were met by a scene of such industry that we were in no doubt our stay would be a short one and we were directed immediately to a loading berth.

The crew studied the quay with some partiality as we went alongside, keenly interested in the nature of our next cargo. All we could see, covering an acre it seemed, were piles of bombs so large it was hard to imagine any aircraft getting off the ground under such weight. The mate's face was a picture of astonishment with just a flicker of that fleeting dismay which we all must have felt.

It was a change to have the American army loading us. Few of the men involved had even seen the sea until they had embarked for Europe. One Sergeant from the Middle West told me they had undergone intensive training in Britain before being sent to North Africa. Now they were working with all kinds of mechanical aids shipped directly from the States and seemed at home in their new skill.

They were very proud of their work rate and pointed out to us a section of the port where motor vehicles - heavy trucks and jeeps - were being assembled on a conveyor belt system which they claimed could cope with as many as 300 a day. I also noticed railway locomotives, also shipped in parts, were being assembled with the same urgent commitment.

One of the setbacks the Allies had met with after the landings was the worn out state of the rolling stock and the tracks which they had hoped to use. The idea that any proportion of our cargo might in the future go by rail was an attractive thought. Even with the speed those Americans displayed I don't think much of it ever did.

The professionals - Nearest the flag locker (from the back):
Maritime Regiment gunners Nevarde, Brewerton, Maloney and Ball.
On the outside: Naval gunners Ginger (against ventilator), Jock and Dave.

We remained at Oran for less than a week and made the most of its abundant facilities. We found an American Red Cross Club in a spacious modern building with a full sized cinema, reading room, music room and snack bar and, if we had had the time, classes for tuition in Spanish and French. The only part strictly reserved for the U.S. Forces was the games room.

As a change from the food aboard, we were able to buy tickets there to be exchanged in two local restaurants for meals appetizingly knocked up from a wide range of army rations. There was also an Allied Forces club in more modest surroundings where we played table tennis.

Though the nearby naval base of Mers-el-Kiber was now occupied by the Royal Navy's Force H, whose battle cruisers *NELSON* and *RODNEY* and the aircraft carrier *FORMIDABLE* had been transferred from Gibraltar, the only British naval presence in Oran seemed to be the trawler base. It was some distance from where we were berthed and as a consequence we got little news from the crews of the minesweepers and small escort ships of the fortunes of other ships in our coastal service.

Oran, we understood, might be our base for some time to come, but it had its material compensations. One was the American PX Store, well stocked with many of the items we had been having to beg. We were running out of soap and those other small necessities Algerian shops so rarely displayed. The PX could provide them in abundance.

Captain Ruig, whose vigilantly apportioned store of Scotch bore diplomatic status transcending on occasions its medicinal usefulness, had as usual made important contacts ashore. It was not long before he gained the entrée to this universal provider for U.S. personnel. Soon he appeared smartly arrayed in the light khaki, cotton drill uniform favoured by the U.S. Navy and officers of its much evident Merchant Marine.

Before leaving we all got passes to that opportune emporium, signing for shirts, towels, trousers, toothpaste and many other items to be debited against our pay. The chief steward was able to obtain tobacco, chocolate and canned beer to sell to us later. When we sailed from that haven of comparative plenty there was an air of cheerfulness aboard which we had not experienced since Christmas.

It was of transient nature. As far as our cargo was concerned we were back to square one. We had loaded a considerable weight of those bombs and a large consignment of high octane petrol in lightweight cans. We were bound for Philippeville again and it was not a mixture to inspire confidence. Peering into the tweendecks whilst the hatchboards were being replaced I saw that one of the bombs was wedged directly under my bunk. Across its broad surface some joker had chalked my name with the injunction: "Not wanted on voyage - Stow away from boilers."

It was a pertinent reminder that the sooner we sailed the sooner we might disencumber ourselves of such embarrassment and the standby signal was not unwelcome. Nothing happened to challenge our composure until we approached Algiers at dawn the following day. We could see tracers in the distance and as we passed, well out to sea, we heard the gunfire as the attack continued.

Our hopes that we could sneak by without being detected seemed to have been fulfilled when no enemy aircraft approached and it was a good omen. Through the long day we clung to our optimism and looked forward to the approaching darkness, but at dusk our luck departed. The alarm sounded as the escorts on our outer flanks opened fire.

Soon we were being attacked from both the land and seaward quarters and the response was impressive. It was a particularly noisy encounter because, soon afterwards, one or more of the escort ships picked up the sounds of U-boat intervention and began dropping depth charges. The deafening noise on the surface of the earsplitting gunfire and roaring engines, and the mighty hammering on our bottom plates achieved a Wagnerian effect which momentarily seized the breath.

There could not have been many planes and no ship was hit, and soon peace was restored, but we were left with the uneasy feeling that the enemy would be back. After a few hours of fitful dozing I went on watch to relieve the lookout and it all started again.

There was a good deal of gunfire, but it was difficult to make out the sounds of attacking aircraft. The firing broke out spasmodically and was wide-ranging as if the convoy was being assailed on the fringes by torpedo aircraft. I took one of the Lewis guns which had been further overhauled, and mounted it on the vegetable locker on the boatdeck, but nothing came our way although our bridge guns opened up occasionally.

There was the sound of depth charges and soon afterwards Joe Stoakes grabbed my arm and pointed towards our port quarter. I could see what appeared to be a large, red fire which flickered and grew and was suddenly transformed into a brilliant fireworks display. We gazed at the brilliant eruption for some time and concluded that one of the escort ships had been hit.

The desultory action continued for some time after that, but gradually died away until all firing ceased. *ODYSSEUS* ploughed on carefully keeping her station in the pitch black of the early morning, her company very much in the dark as to what potential danger she had again successfully eluded.

We reached Philippeville at daylight and our pleasure at getting in safely was soon eclipsed by the great delight of learning that the ship's first mail in three months was about to be delivered. By that time we had almost given up hope of ever seeing any.

It was appropriately our radio officer, Jack Ridler, who brought it back from the shore with an expression on his face that signalled the good news from far along the quay. He had steadfastly been trying to track it down for several weeks and now returned in triumph. As he patiently attended to its distribution, curbing the natural desire to grab his own share, he was undoubtedly the most popular communications specialist in the western Mediterranean.

It was a sensitive occasion because some of the Dutch crew held little hope of getting any tidings from the homeland they had not seen for nearly three years. It was one of the reasons why those of us anxious to hear from our homes in Britain had never made any undue fuss over the delay in our mail. It wasn't through any general discussion, just an instinctive realisation that such reminders might hurt.

As it happened many of the Nederlanders got letters from friends and families they had become closely associated with during their exile. There were also the cryptic Red Cross communications bearing terse messages confirming that those dear to them in Holland were surviving. For some there was no mail, but perhaps there never would have been. They did not allow any feelings they might have had to intrude on the general elation.

```
Bounds in Philipville.          Verboden plaatsen in Philipville.

The Arab quarter is out of bounds to all forces.

De hoerebuurt is verboden voor iedereen.

The following cafes and estaminets are out of bounds to all forces.

The volgende cafes en openbare vermakelijkheden zijn verboden voor iederen.

Bar Robert        Rue Clemenceau.
Cafe de la marine  ,,    ,,
Cafe de la renessance ,,  ,,
Cafe Mamon          ,,   ,,
Cafe Napolion    Rue Valee.  ,,
Bar Clemenceau   ,,    ..

                                    Master.
```

Entertainment ashore was limited

I noticed that the latest letters were several weeks old and rejoiced in the thought that others were still chasing us round. It was something else to look forward to.

It was a light hearted crew who uncovered the hatches and swung out the weighty beams to begin the discharging of our lethal load. The soldiers involved in that arduous task, assuming no doubt that we had been celebrating some special occasion such as the Captain's birthday, grinned broadly and were happy for us.

There were no attacks from the air to interrupt the work which went on quickly, but our brief visit was not unmarred by the enemy's attention or the tragedy in its train. Whilst we lay there the trawler *STRONSAY* was destroyed by a mine, with the loss of most of her crew, just outside the port. She had been the ship for whose crew we had baked some bread on a previous visit.

There was a special relationship because members of *ODYSSEUS*'s crew had witnessed her launching at a Scottish yard only a year before. She was not the only ship and crew we mourned that week. Two days later, off the cape which sheltered the westerly approaches to the port, the mine-sweeping trawler *TERVANI* was hit by a submarine torpedo and sank with heavy loss.

It confirmed the view that most of us had formed that such minor warships, many of them requisitioned from peacetime fishing fleets and carrying much the same crews, had the toughest job of all and often the most perilous along that dangerous coast. Their size seemed out of all proportion to the important role they served.

Before we sailed *ODYSSEUS* faced a domestic crisis arising from the violent effect of the local liquor on our normally well behaved Arabian. Most of the local bars and cafes had been put out of bounds to all forces, as was the Arab quarter. Yet it would have been difficult for those responsible for enforcing the ban to distinguish between our most recent crew member and many of the residents of the Rue Clemenceau and the Rue Valee where such premises existed.

From such excursions he returned a changed man, no longer the urbane, smiling conversationalist and engaging raconteur. He had a wild look in his eyes and the determination to quarrel. In fact he was a menace, screaming and shouting on the deck and in the firemen's fo'c'sle until forcibly restrained and deposited in his bunk.

Once he picked up a knife and it took six of the crew to disarm him, and Joe Stoakes volunteered to keep watch in case he awoke and went in search of the many knives we had carefully hidden. In the morning he was a contrite character, embarrassingly penitent and diligent with the work in hand. He clearly had a problem and so did we.

It was taken care of in a way which was probably inevitable, yet managed to arouse some degree of sympathy among those whose sleep he had disturbed. He was brought aboard looking considerably cowed, chained to a gendarme who had no intention of handing him over. He merely wanted to collect his papers on the way to the lock-up. We were told he had run amok and attacked two American seamen in the town.

Jim, who was always slow to condemn such human frailty, but had used a heavy hand to suppress its worst effects, tried to slip him some cash and cigarettes before he was hauled away, but he shook his head and indicated that it would only be confiscated. He had a sad look on his face as he bade us farewell, the expression of a man who knew he had blown it. There was just the trace of a smile when someone said consolingly: "At least they can't deport you to France."

It took us nearly three days to get back to Oran mainly because of the slowness of some of the ships that were showing their age or growing need for engine repairs. If we had had bad weather to confront, or some other testing diversion from that fickle quarter it would have come as a relief. Steaming along at no more than seven knots on occasions, in conditions ideal for enemy attack, made the anticipation as nervously exhausting as the event.

Ironically it was in the comparative safety of that seemingly well sheltered port that *ODYSSEUS* got her next testing from the elements. The French pilot had not been misleading us when he had referred, rather proudly I thought, to the suddenness, scale and duration of local storms. When we had arrived it was believed that we might be diverted to one or other of the nearby smaller ports of Arzew or Mostaganem for a transhipment cargo.

Consequently we moored in the outer harbour with both anchors down and our stern ropes made fast to the mole in traditional Mediterranean style. It was a broad, high mole sweeping out into the bay like some impregnable bastion.

On the seaward side of this mighty protective arm was an outer reef of large boulders, piled against the wall to break the first fury of any angry seas. It was a storm guard to inspire confidence, yet when the barometer dropped significantly we took extraordinary measures to prepare for a sudden blow and I was reminded that the *ODYSSEUS* had spent much of her peaceful working life in those waters.

As the wind rose we put out more stern moorings until eventually we had four from each quarter holding us to the mole. Two of them were wreckers, heavy cable-laid ropes shackled to wires which had to be manhandled from the rope locker to be taken aft. With so small a deck crew it was laborious work. Then the Captain and the mate showed much concern about the number of heavy lighters, some laden with timber, which had broken adrift and threatened to bear down on us.

As no-one else seemed to be doing anything to capture them we spent the next few hours rounding them up and mooring them as best we could further along the wall. By this time the wind was rising and its effect on those vessels moored across the harbour beyond the shelter of the mole was all too evident. That night we kept watch in turns on the poop with an anxious eye on our moorings as the wind pressure rapidly increased.

When I took over the watch at midnight I was astonished at the height of the sea which, in places, was now sweeping over the mole with its crests breaking in the harbour. It was a dramatic sight and an unsettling sound.

When I had last looked, in daylight, there had been a hut below the highest rampart opposite us, a shelter for some soldiers in charge of smoke screen burners. There was now no sign of their cabin which must have been swept away. With any luck they had been withdrawn before the storm had reached its height. At one time I thought I heard a voice crying out from somewhere on the wall, but it was probably imagination. Under those conditions there was nothing we could have done to help.

Further out along the mole had been a Bofors gun emplacement, but its position was by that time a smother of exploding spray when it was not completely engulfed. I hoped its crew had been remembered in time. It was whilst I was pondering on their fate that one of our stern ropes parted with a crack that might have been a gunshot.

It was the second one to have gone since nightfall and all hands had been turned out in an attempt to replace the first. It had been unsuccessful and conditions were now infinitely worse. There was no hope of launching a boat and no other way of getting a line to the shore. Even if that had been possible the sight of the great wave crests sweeping its masonry with such force excluded it as suicidal.

It was not surprising that two of our moorings had carried away. With the ship's counter rising giddily to the force of every wave that thundered over the mole, and plunging down again as the bow caught the upward thrust, it seemed only a matter of time before they all went.

I checked the remaining moorings at these points where the frictional damage might weaken them most and then called out the third mate and the Bo'sun. There was little they could do but help me renew some of the chafing gear with strips of old canvas as the stern dipped and the ropes and wires momentarily slackened. Mistiming the sudden tautening would have been a sure way of losing a finger or getting one crushed.

The Bo'sun and I rigged up a canvas shelter and crouched behind it, avoiding the worst of the blast and listening for ominous noises against the tempestuous tumult. A crashing from within the harbour told us that the barges had broken away again and it was occasionally possible to make out the shape of one against the yeasty face of the waves which swept over the barrage at one minute intervals.

There was not much we could do about them either and we were both alarmed when one of the runaway craft, heavily laden with timber, charged down on us out of the darkness and crashed into our plates. It struck just beneath our counter and threatened to damage our rudder until, by some quirk of the turbulence surrounding us, it swung neatly round and settled comfortably along our port quarter.

Because the sounds from inside the harbour were being snatched away by the storm it was difficult to make out what disasters might be happening further away. But we now and then heard the urgent hoot of distant sirens.

Soon after 3.00am I picked up another cry from the direction of the mole and this time I had no doubt it was a human voice. Soon I made out the figure of a man clinging to a ledge on the lower level of the sea swept wall. He was bedraggled and seemed exhausted, but comparatively secure, having found some overhanging stonework to protect him from the full force of the powerful cascade.

We weighted a long heaving line and the Bo'sun and I took it in turns in trying to reach him with it. The Bo'sun with his powerful throw landed the end of it at least twice within his reach, but he showed no inclination to hold on to it. I got a megaphone from the bridge and tried to persuade him to pull it in as we had made a stronger rope fast to it, yet he seemed disinclined to co-operate.

Perhaps he was past caring or, more likely, did not fancy taking his chances among the dangerous flotsam in the watery ferment separating him from the safety *ODYSSEUS* offered. The Bo'sun was disappointed. Although he was much concerned about the man, his first concern was for the ship and he had been intending to enlist the aid of the castaway and any companions in replacing one of our missing moorings.

There was nothing else we could do and an hour later, soaked to the skin with my oilskins clinging like damp blotting paper, I went in search of some dry gear. At the first streaks of daylight I knew we would all have much to do.

About dawn the violence of the storm seemed to have passed its peak and our first consideration was to attend to our moorings in case its full fury returned. It was still impossible to launch a boat with any safety, but the problem of establishing contact with the mole was soon solved. There was a short jetty jutting from it further along, against which some of the unattended lighters had become trapped by the wind and waves.

By using one of the fugitive barges now hammering against our bows, and releasing it with a working party aboard to drift down upon those grinding against each other at the jetty, we were able to bridge the gap. There was no sign of life on the wall opposite and we hoped that the man we had seen there earlier had been able to make his way along to the shore safely.

There was no sign of the cabin once occupied by him and his companions either, or their smoke making equipment, until we scanned the harbour and saw their caboose floating like some half submerged Noah's ark in the stormy waters. Waves were still breaking over the wall, but the third mate, Bo'sun and one of the sailors picked their moment and scrambled along to the stone bollards holding our moorings.

They got drenched but by hugging the wall avoided being washed away. They took our lines, hauled out two more ropes and restored the situation with admirable alacrity before making their way back to the jetty. At least, two of them did.

The third mate who was more of a gymnast than I suspected chose an acrobatic withdrawal, swinging himself out on to one of the mooring ropes and then using his hands and legs to make a spectacular crossing of which Tarzan would have been proud. It was a performance which would have won a cheer in the circus ring and it earned our applause as he was hauled over the rail.

The mate immediately organised all hands at his disposal to impound the runaway barges pitching and rolling around the ship, which we secured on either side to form a formidable fender against any ship that might drift our way. Those on the barge at the jetty were winched back on the coir rope to which it was attached and, as the storm continued to abate, we began to feel snug again.

All around were scenes of stress. The damaged Cunarder *SCYTHIA* which had been lying alongside the mole now lay well away from the wall, her upperdecks showing evidence of the battering they had taken. Many of the wreck buoys which had marked the positions of sunken ships were missing or out of position and there were many small craft and some larger ones extricating themselves from the dangerous areas into which they had been driven by the storm.

When conditions had recovered sufficiently for us to move in to a loading berth, the American soldiers who cast off our stern moorings brought good news. All those caught on the mole had somehow survived and been taken off safely.

Our pleasure at being again within reach of the well organised facilities beyond the quayside was diminished considerably when we saw the many drums of petrol waiting there to be loaded. We felt happier when the U.S. Army Lieutenant in charge of the operation told us they were not for us, yet there was something furtive in the way he clutched his clipboard to his chest as if protecting top-secret information of great sensitivity.

Perhaps he was trying to be kind, for later on we realised that our cargo was the mixture as before and he was careful not to catch our eyes as we watched his men packing mortar bombs in fibre containers around the drums of aviation fuel in our tweendecks. Again it was a consignment bound for Philippeville, but this time Sergeant Bunce was not going with us.

I for one was sorry because I had enjoyed his intrepid presence. Under the constrictions of our somewhat limited defence it could not have been easy for our veteran warhorse to show the enemy it was taking on the fighting traditions of the Royal Marines whenever it made a pass at us. He had not done badly though, and kept us amused.

When he handed over to a younger man, a D.E.M.S. petty officer of philosophical disposition, he wished us well and, intriguing to the last, managed to leave us with the impression that he was needed for some more tactical role. We took to his successor right away. For one thing he had a camera.

CHAPTER TEN

Shortly before we sailed Jack Ridler, who had been ashore chasing up the mail, returned triumphantly with some more letters. It was my birthday and I was astonished to realise that one of the envelopes he handed to me obviously contained a card. Later when I found the opportunity to open it I discovered it was a Christmas card which had taken two months to arrive.

It was nonetheless welcome and in time for a celebration without us having to turn back the calendar. Things were otherwise back to normal we soon found. As we steamed out to join the convoy newly arrived from Gibraltar a distant pillar of smoke and the sound of a torpedo striking home brought the situation back into focus.

It was a tanker that had been hit, the British ship *SEMINOLE*, which we later learned had survived the explosion and made port. She was just a stationary smudge astern as we joined that part of the convoy continuing east towards Algiers. Approaching that port we got a signal to fall out of line and head inside, a change of destination which surprised us and was greeted with undisguised enthusiasm.

Sparks and Eric and I had some unfinished business to attend to in Algiers. The Bo'sun, on behalf of some members of the Dutch crew, had discussed with us their concern over one particular elderly member who they felt was now suffering the strain. Not that he had complained or was ever likely to. They felt it was unfair that a man of his age should be engaged at all in the operation to which we were committed.

There were one or two others approaching his age on the engineroom side. The complete lack of information about the length of our involvement, of which few of us were in any real doubt, only added for them to the anxiety of uncertainty. We were approached because of the language difficulty and it was thought we might have the best chance of getting some definite information through the official sources ashore.

Our promise to consult the Sea Transport people which we had not been able to fulfil on our last visit had not been forgotten. There were other matters including that of our mail which we felt could be usefully discussed. There were also a good many rumours which we had picked up from other ships concerning our future. To have them either confirmed or scotched would be a timely exercise.

It was an interesting exploration and illuminating, though not entirely in the way we had hoped. We found the Sea Transport officer in a building almost at the other end of the waterfront and received a sympathetic hearing. He wore a commander's uniform and we knew instinctively that we were treading a well worn path and were about to be deflected.

Our artless requests did not seem to surprise him in the least and clearly he had heard it all before. It was easy to see he had his own problems and indeed, if we had talked with him longer, our sympathy with them might quickly have outweighed any concern we had for our own. He soon suggested that the Consul General's office was the place for us to go and most obligingly phoned through to arrange our appointment.

Before we left he confided that Admiral Sir Andrew Cunningham, Commander-in-Chief of the Allied naval forces in the Mediterranean, had taken a personal interest in the welfare of such ships as ours. He quoted from a stirring New Year's message to their crews in which the Admiral thanked them specially, and seemed genuinely taken aback when we revealed that it had so far not reached the crew of *ODYSSEUS*.

One of us, either Eric or Jack, said as he rose to hand us on: "Perhaps it will catch up when we find the rest of our mail", and he gave a wry smile. It was turning out to be an interesting afternoon, a pleasantly stimulating contrast to shipboard routine and its uninformed speculation, and it was agreeably rounded off by our courteous reception at the British Consulate.

The official who saw us comfortably seated was, I think, anticipating something more than our simple and modest pursuit of a few elementary facts to take back aboard. He talked to us like a Dutch uncle and quickly launched into an encouraging summary of plans he claimed were already in hand to improve our somewhat spartan life style.

He spoke of a scheme to give members of crews breaks ashore when circumstances permitted and surprised us by revealing that soon there might be fresh ships on their way out to relieve those presently operating the coastal supply service. Such was his apparent concern that we lapped it up, but listened even more intently when he let it drop that the commodores of the coastal convoys had been complaining about the speed of some of the small vessels involved.

It was a genuine danger to the larger, faster vessels making those runs, something we had been aware of, just as we were wide awake to the fact that the available escorts were stretched to their limit. The gloomiest speculation aboard had centred on how long it would be before those ships too slow to keep up would be sent off in small clutches with minimum cover, easy prey for the predators.

It was a reality we were soon to face and being brought back to earth was at least some confirmation of our own interpretations of the way in which things were going. Yet we returned aboard with sufficient optimistic news to bring cheer in some quarters, confiding our grimmer thoughts only to the Bo'sun and Jim and those members of the crew who would have arrived at the same conclusion in any case.

There was another call I had to make in Algiers. Though my back seemed to be making good progress and I had for some time been taking my full part in the work of the ship, the Scots army doctor had made me promise to see him again when the opportunity offered.

He was concerned I think to keep an eye on my condition because I had had no X-rays. He was a conscientious man to whom I was grateful and I was disappointed when the orderly I knew told me he had been transferred the day before to care for the medical needs of German and Italian prisoners somewhere inland. He must have been very popular if the hung-over atmosphere of that medical aid post, following his send-off, was anything to go by.

His successor was more formal and had yet to develop a good quayside manner. He didn't even grin when, after giving me a thorough examination and making many notes, he wrote out his instructions on the appropriate form restricting me to light duties until further notice. As the *ODYSSEUS* had no such job description I put it away where it could be best forgotten.

Our brief stay in Algiers, which remained unexplained, may have had something to do with our convoy speed. It set a new pattern for our coastal shuttle and we hoped it was a strategy to minimise waiting time in the more vulnerable discharging ports. That theory seemed to be confirmed when we reached Philippeville where we went alongside immediately to be unloaded.

We had just missed a heavy raid and the soldiers who were quickly at grips with our cargo told us that a bomb had fallen where we were berthed. They were not sure whether it had detonated or not, but were treating the matter with such unconcern we did likewise, hoping it was a dud.

The stones of the quay bore several daubs of white paint indicating where bombs, some dropped from cargo slings, lay dormant in the harbour bed. As most were without fuses their recovery was sometimes delayed and not, it seemed, considered urgent. Fortunately with virtually no rise and fall of tide there was little danger of any ship settling on one.

When we left it was in the company of one other ship of about our size. Our escort, as usual, was a naval trawler and we expected to meet a west-bound convoy coming up from Bone. Captain Ruig had said nothing, but it gradually dawned on us that our fears that one day we might be relegated to such minimal protection, had materialised. It came as something of a shock nonetheless, to realise that our modest trio comprised the convoy.

All we could do about it was to hope for the worst of visibility. We prayed for low cloud, thick fog or heavy rain, none of which seemed at all likely. With our puny air defence and negligible protection against any German or Italian submarine, very likely to be lying in wait, our only consolation was that we had disgorged our most recent eruptive load.

No doubt the crews of the other two small vessels were praying as well for soon the morning sky had darkened and nature presented us with a satisfying mixture of all three. The rain squalls made it difficult at time to see our consorts and throughout the afternoon the cloud base continued unbroken at an altitude few flyers would choose to penetrate.

By nightfall the trawler had signalled her intention of taking us into Bougie and we arrived there before midnight after a painfully slow journey. All we saw of that much battered port was the brief flicker of a dim light on the sea wall indicating the entrance. We were away again before dawn continuing our snails' pace to the westward appreciating all the more, with every hour, why any anxious commodore would object to the inclusion in his convoy of our consort ship.

At times she seemed capable of no more than six knots and, light as she was, against the wind she was sometimes only making five. At the wheel my ears were assailed by the mate's frequent and frustrated instruction to the engineroom of: "Drie klappen minder!" as he reduced our speed. Such constant reduction to the revolutions of our screw was necessary if we were to remain in company and the watchkeeper in the trawler's engineroom must have found it equally trying.

We were not without sympathy for the crew of the other ship, a Norwegian I think, whose anxieties in manning so unsuitable a vessel in such hazardous conditions must have made every trip a nightmare. Fortunately the weather conditions remained overcast and bleak for much of our journey, but we were relieved when the night again enclosed us.

We reached Algiers in the middle of the night and groped our way blindly into port, luckily without mishap. In the morning we learned there was mail waiting for us, an encouraging indication that our representation ashore had not fallen on deaf ears.

On our second day alongside there was another surprise which brought particular pleasure to our Dutch shipmates. Our Nederlands ensign was frequently changed and never allowed to remain blemished by smoke or the weather, yet I was surprised when the second mate produced a new one and told me to hoist it in place of the perfectly presentable bunting flying at our stern.

When the senior Jacob saw what I was doing and suggested we were about to receive a Royal visit I took it as a joke about the tweede stuurman's punctilious ways. Perhaps if Joe Stoakes, Eric and myself had not been clearing up the dunnage in number three hold we might have noticed that several of the officers were wearing their best uniforms and with other uncommonly smart members of the ship's company were idling on deck trying to keep clean.

When Jacob Ouwehand poked his head over the hatch coaming and shouted down to us that Prince Bernhard was coming aboard we took it as another of his jokes - an attempt to get us to climb out off the hold, the sort of trick of which he was fond. It was only when the Bo'sun came along some time later to ask why we had not come up that we realised Jacob had been in earnest. The Bo'sun thought it was very funny and roared with laughter as we watched the Royal visitor, dressed in airforce uniform, climb into his car to be driven off.

The Prince, who had stayed but briefly, had shaken a lot of clean hands and boosted morale considerably by his visit, particularly by his assurance that the *ODYSSEUS* was soon to be relieved.

Though we did not get to shake hands with the Prince we, and all the crew, reaped a benefit of which he was most probably unaware. It may have been in the cook's mind that we would be having a Royal guest for lunch and, to his credit, he had done his best to make it a

105

memorable occasion. As a result we had the best midday meal we had tasted since Christmas.

Not many finished the rather unusual chocolate pudding, but the mood by then was too cheerful for carping criticism and for all we knew the Prince may have missed out. It might have been his favourite. Any disappointment the cook might have felt was soon alleviated by the heady sensation of fleeting popularity.

A more enduring bonus came our way when Eric and I visited the Strick Line ship *HUNDUSTAN* and came away with armfuls of books and other reading material of which we were woefully short. She had been damaged by bombs in Bone back in December and our benefactors had some sympathy for our situation.

There were two disappointments. The first arose from a visit we made to a Royal Navy stores depot where we presented official passes and hoped to buy some items of warm gear for chilly night watches. The duffel coats we had been promised at Milford Haven had never been delivered. We were not well received and, after being passed down the line, left empty handed without so much as a pair of seaboot stockings.

The second was much more of a blow. Jim van Ommeren who had seemed under the weather for some days had eventually been persuaded to visit the army medical post along the quay, mainly on my recommendation. He did not look very happy when he returned and told us he was being sent to a military hospital where he would be kept for observations. It was the thought of the regimentation that worried him most, and we did our best to persuade him the rest would do him good.

We had no doubt that he would take the first opportunity to discharge himself, but there was gloom in the fo'c'sle when we sailed. It lifted briefly when we realised that the part cargo we had taken aboard, a consignment of steel plates for the repair of some ship or other, was destined for Casablanca. It immediately built up our hopes of making a trip back into the Atlantic and seeing a new port, only to learn it was to be transhipped at Oran.

I was spinning the spokes of the wheel and keeping an eye on the compass bowl, and wondering how Jim was getting on when there came a sickening explosion. Closed in as I was it was impossible to see which ship had been hit, knowing only by the steadiness of our course and our even keel that it wasn't us. The feel of the ship had a soothing effect at such moments and being at the helm seemed much the best place.

From the violence of the explosion and from the activity on the wings of the bridge I guessed it was close and probably just astern of us or in an adjacent column. There had been no aircraft alarm and the culprit had to be a submarine.

A few minutes later when my relief had taken over I looked astern and saw the *OCEAN SEAMAN*, a war replacement ship not long away from the builder's yard, listing heavily and obviously doomed, with one escort standing by. Elsewhere the hunt was on for her attacker, though I feared she must have got away to lie in the depths and prepare to strike again. At the convoy's modest speed it would be many hours before we reached Oran and there was an anxious night ahead.

Wartime picture of Oran dominated by the 16th Century fort standing sentinel between the commercial port and the naval harbour of Mers-el-Kebir beyond the hill.

It passed without incident and the day dawned bright and clear as many eyes in many ships scrutinized a cellophane sea for the least trace of an enemy presence. Towards noon the convoy was off the

Gulf of Arzew and those ships which would leave it to enter Oran were keeping the commodore vessel in view for the signal to break away. The underlying fear of lurking danger was the only shadow to darken the serene splendour of the Middle Sea.

The third mate who had joined me to take a bearing off the land was relaxed and happily reminiscent about the delights of trading in such waters in the almost forgotten days of peace. The unsynchronised sounds of eight bells being struck as other ships changed their watches was savagely drowned by the violent detonation of a torpedo finding its mark, somewhere to starboard and on our quarter.

I did not look round immediately for, if the submarine was inshore, there might have been other outward bound missiles on their way. But there were no telltale bubble trails.

As I turned to scan the water to seaward there came a second explosion and the sea erupted against the plates of an American freighter on our starboard hand, partly concealing it in the cascade of water and drifting smoke. She had been high in the water, one of the ships heading for home for another military cargo. Suddenly she heeled over so violently that her bilge keel caught the blaze of the sun to flash its own dire signal of distress.

Astern of her in another column the first stricken vessel, another Liberty ship flying the Stars and Stripes, listed as, forlornly, her buoyancy diminished by the minute. Both were near enough to Oran to hold out some hope of salvage, but I guessed that neither would see any port again. We got no chance to witness their fate. By that time the other ships in the convoy were swinging away from the land to present as small a target as possible to any further salvos.

There was also the diversion of a swooping aircraft, easily recognised as an American fighter. Instantly gun crews had swung their weapons, only to hold their fire. Any plane passing over a convoy was normally fair game and it seemed that the American pilot had spotted something he thought we should know about. His reward was a burst of gunfire from one ship strictly abiding by the rules and, as the shell splinters hissed into the sea around us, the pilot made a hasty retreat.

The escort ships, few enough, faced a difficult decision. It was a large convoy mainly consisting of valuable tonnage bound for the Strait of Gibraltar. With a U-boat about and two casualties to attend to it was an illustration of the problems the Royal Navy faced and of how thinly its units had to be spread. Hunting U-boats was a time consuming operation and, though we heard depth charges being dropped astern, they were probably only to keep the enemy down.

The convoy pressed on, depleted in cargo ships and in escort, and when the signal came for us to break off for Oran we were glad to hear the telegraph ring for a boost in speed as we willingly departed. Several other ships went in with us, but *ODYSSEUS* led the race. In spite of our recent experience moored to the mole we were happy to be back there discharging our cargo into some of the lighters we had previously fought with in the storm.

The rumour was that our next cargo was bound for Bone which, for special reasons, had not had many peaceful nights or days for that matter, since the Allies arrived there. Yet the idea was not without its appeal. If we were to continue steaming up and down the coast some new scenery at the other end struck most of the crew as a welcome change.

There was some elation aboard too when the Bo'sun announced that we had to unrig the jumbo derrick, a weighty spar whose giant blocks and monstrous tackle we had spent a laborious day assembling soon after our first arrival in Algiers.

Some of the Dutch members of the crew took it as a sure sign that Prince Bernhard's assurance would soon come to pass, an indication that perhaps our next trip down the coast would be our last. The anticipated invasion of Europe across the English Channel had been much discussed and the triumphant return to their homeland was something they did not want to miss.

The Bo'sun knew better, but was careful not to shatter their hopes. I had overheard him talking with the mate and knew it was just another of that gentleman's ideas for keeping the deck crew busy. Like all first officers since the beginning of time his waking hours were occupied in thinking of jobs to keep us hard at work in port and dismantling the jumbo derrick, which we had never used, nicely took care of another day.

Without realising it he had contrived to raise the crew's spirits for once and even Jacob Harteveld, who was well aware of the mate's inclination, talked happily for a time about his wartime home in Essex. I took it as a compliment when he asked me if I would stay with the ship when we got back. Yet it was a difficult question to answer because by then I had become even more firmly convinced that, the enemy permitting, the *ODYSSEUS* would be among the last ships of all to sail for home.

There was one man who might have put an end to some of the speculation, but the master of the ship had, so far as I knew, made no public comment. Indeed, over the passing months there were those among the crew, including myself, who had formed the opinion that if it came to the point Captain Ruig might even resist any decision to return his ship to home waters. In spite of her perilous occupation her present employment seemed to satisfy his mood.

For him the Mediterranean had its compensations between trips. From the limited conversations on watch I knew it was an area he had enjoyed in pre-war days. He had friends ashore whose hospitality he was able to return, which created some social life, particularly in Algiers and Oran. But mainly, I think, he had an unfathomable pride in his command, a belief perhaps that the *ODYSSEUS* was playing an important role in a war the Allies were at last winning.

Though he was too taciturn ever to say as much in my presence, he gave every other evidence of a strong faith in her survival. I had little doubt that so long as she retained a useful turn of speed he would declare for staying on.

We had not always been lucky in crew replacements, especially in the stokehold. The candidate recruited from the Algiers pool, to succeed the Arab removed by the gendarmerie, had turned out to be a disaster. Faced with a pile of coal and a hungry furnace he lost all stamina and the ship lost its head of steam. His rapid demotion to trimmer brought joyful advancement to elderly Vrolyk who, long before, had been relegated to the bunkers.

But the new man apparently became just as much in arrears in that department and lost all popularity with his watchmates. For sympathy he turned to his fellow countrymen in the sailors' fo'c'sle until they realised what the black gang had had to put up with both on and off watch. By mutual consent it was decided in Oran that he would go.

He was a pretty hopeless case with a mean disposition and the news of his impending departure was greeted with relief. We looked forward to seeing the last of him, not realising that we hadn't seen the worst of him. He went ashore on the eve of his signing off and when he had not returned by nightfall we rather hoped we would not see him again.

I was on another watch later that night and was in the galley making myself some coffee when I heard what I thought was a cry for help. Making my way to the poop I peered into the darkness and then heard a more distinct shout of desperation. It was just possible to make out a drooping figure hanging on to one of our mooring ropes near the foot of some stone steps.

We did not have a boat in the water and I got a heaving line and was making it fast to a lifebuoy when a sailor on a nearby Norwegian ship shouted across that they had a skiff. He quickly sculled it over and soon enough was pulling the soggy, struggling bundle aboard. When he delivered his seemingly ungrateful passenger alongside I realised it was our missing trimmer, mainly from his whining abuse.

It would have been difficult to recognise him otherwise because he had been well and truly stirred about in the oily scum under the mole and looked as if he had just crawled out of a tar drum. His rescuer had collected his share of it and was glad to hand him over, though it was no easy job getting him up the jacob's ladder.

It was no simple matter getting a grip on him and I was coated in oil by the time I had got him on to the deck. He seemed half drowned, but obviously did not need any artificial resuscitation, an emetic perhaps and certainly a good bath. He was wearing a suit which I stripped off him and threw on the hatch. Then I did my best to get the worst of the oil off his face and neck, arms and legs where it had oozed in under his clothing.

Twice I went down to the engineroom to get some hot water from the condenser sump, and eventually wrapped him in some blankets and got him into his bunk. By that time the other occupants of the firemen's fo'c'sle were awake and complaining about the mess he had left on the white painted bulkheads. They were still complaining loudly long after he had fallen asleep with the fixed grimace of a man who had consoled himself well and perhaps got his own back.

The next morning he smashed our "Land of Hope and Glory" record and, abandoning his suit, left us without explaining how a man with such unwilling muscular function could ever have hoped to get back aboard using our stern mooring. He also left us wondering how and why he had been sent to North Africa in a relief party in the first place.

CHAPTER ELEVEN

When *ODYSSEUS* sailed for Bone in the last week of March there was a distant air of optimism among her crew, a cheerfulness tinged with curiosity as to what our extended beat, which would take us a few more miles to the east, might add to our experience. It was as if we had got our second wind and with it some latent desire for further adventure.

Our cargo, so far as we had taken stock, consisted mainly of mortar ammunition urgently needed no doubt by the First Army, consisting of British, French and American units, which was striving hard in the mountainous Tunisian hinterland to compress a fiercely resisting enemy. It had had its setbacks earlier in the year when German armoured thrusts had threatened the supply lines we were helping to feed.

Such alarms had not escaped our notice on one of our visits to Philippeville when, for a couple of days until the situation was restored, we had felt the excitement in the air. Now the enemy, expelled from Libya by the advance of the Eighth Army, had abandoned the Mareth Line below the Gulf of Gabes and was in danger of losing its supply ports of Sfax and Sousse below Cape Bon.

How long it might yet take to squeeze the Axis forces into submission was still anyone's guess, but the realisation that soon only Bizerta and Tunis might remain in their hands made our own close commitment an added spur.

Though the fortunes of war on land were now reaching a slow but successful climax the enemy intervention over, on and under the sea continued with the same determination and element of surprise. Added to it perhaps was a new spirit of desperation in a still powerful enemy with air and sea bases unhealthily close across the narrow waters separating Africa from Sicily, Sardinia and southern Italy.

It was a gauntlet each convoy ran in which the enemy had many chances of striking home once any shipping activity had been spotted. Night or day seemed to make no difference, though occasionally weather conditions could be an ally. The cloak of darkness was first choice though for those ships, specially selected for their turn of speed and troop carrying capacity, and it served them well.

The key ships between Algiers and Bone which we only glimpsed occasionally in port were the modern Dutch motor vessels

KONIGIN EMMA and her twin *PRINSES BEATRIX*, which in the year before the war had been built to grace the Harwich to the Hook of Holland and the Folkestone to Flushing sea routes, and the two British twins from the Irish Sea ferry route, Burns & Laird's *ROYAL SCOTSMAN* and *ROYAL ULSTERMAN*.

Between them they must have moved several divisions of troops along that dangerous route to the fighting line without loss. Separately, but also at night, another small group of special craft had been successfully delivering urgently needed tools of war. They carried tanks and their crews, mainly to Bone.

Three of them were converted tankers, ingeniously adapted for the purpose. The fourth was our old friend the *EMPIRE DACE*, the vehicle ferry whose future employment had so puzzled us when she evoked our concern during the heavy weather of our outward voyage the previous November. Since then she had contributed handsomely to the Allied cause, transporting a large number of armoured vehicles and trucks to within a short distance of where they were vitally needed.

The tankers, in whose company she appeared such an ugly duckling, were the *BACHAQUERO, MISOA* and the slightly smaller *TASAJERA* whose normal employment was carrying oil from the wells in Lake Maracaibo in Venezuela for transhipment at Aruba. They had been fitted with bow doors and ramps and were a stopgap until the Allies could produce the custom built LST's we were eventually to see in considerable numbers.

They had barely half the speed of the troop carriers, but between them they could move seventy or more of the heaviest tanks, together with more than eight hundred men, in one trip. It was a serious blow to the enemy that they had managed to deliver safely every consignment.

So far the *ODYSSEUS* had managed to do the same, but her crew was still keeping its fingers crossed as we plodded even more slowly towards our objective. There was a sense of relief when the night closed in on us and we could look back on an uneventful day, but our luck was soon to be tested again.

In the half light of the early morning, as we were approaching Algiers, the hunters spotted us and the throb of encircling aircraft brought back the familiar tension. They were torpedo planes and very quickly the sky was alive with tracers and the burst of heavier fire.

ORPHEUS (1,000 grt) - the smallest of the K.N.S.M. steamers serving in North African waters photographed at Amsterdam before Holland was invaded.
(Courtesy of Nedlloyd)

The attackers had the advantage at low altitude in the poor light and, picking their opportunities, made elusive targets.

It could have been described as a running battle if the convoy had been capable of greater speed. It seemed long drawn out as the attacks developed on different sections of the convoy attracting the fire of those ships which could defend themselves without endangering their consorts. As it grew lighter the assaults seemed to become more concentrated perhaps because our assailants were having no luck, so far as we could judge, and the approach of full daylight would make them more vulnerable.

Not far from us towards the rear of the convoy was another ship whose prominent Dutch flag had caught our attention the day before. She was a new motorship, *PRINS WILLEM III*, making her first voyage along the coast following her arrival at Gibraltar. Her guns had been particularly active. It must have been getting on for 6.00am when the shock of an exploding torpedo from her direction proclaimed the enemy's success at last.

It was possible to make out the bare details of her distress. She had been hit in the stern where her crew's quarters were and her boatdeck looked a shambles. Soon the drastic alteration of her trim served to obscure any further view of the plight of those aboard and we sailed on, relieved that she had not gone up in flames or erupted violently.

We had seen another Dutch ship, the *ORPHEUS*, of our size and vintage and belonging to the same company, apparently engaged in rescue work. There was also an escort ship standing by as we steamed away. We were to learn later that eleven members of her crew, including one gunner, had lost their lives and that others were wounded. The *PRINS WILLEM III* did not sink right away.

She was loaded with ammunition and aviation fuel in barrels and cans and an attempt was made by her master and members of her crew to get her into Algiers with the help of the Hunt class destroyer *WHEATLAND* and the tug *HENGIST*. She capsized and sank after being abandoned some hours later.

Confirmation that the enemy was now using a more sinister type of torpedo that followed an ever decreasing circular track came through the same source, a member of the crew of the *ORPHEUS* I think. She had taken some of the wounded survivors into Algiers where, that night, German planes had launched five such missiles. One had completed the destruction of an already crippled cargo ship, hitting her in that part of the hull where she had already received a torpedo blast.

Others had done damage ashore, one hitting a pier on which there was a Bofors gun emplacement. Its army crew escaped injury, but were not without indignation. Another which hit the mole was recovered intact which was a bonus for the torpedo experts.

The Hunt-class destroyer WHEATLAND which, with the Naval
tug HENGIST, attempted to tow the torpedoed Dutch
cargo ship PRINS WILLEM III into Algiers Bay.
(Courtesy of W.S.S.)

Whilst such distractions were exciting those ashore our fleet continued its painfully slow progress towards that area in which so many convoy battles had been fought since June 1940 when Mussolini entered the war and, only days later, Britain lost the support of the French navy and its strategic Mediterranean bases.

From their Sicilian airfields the Italian and German forces dominated the approaches to Cape Bon and the narrow channel beyond. Attempts to sustain Malta became desperate gambles in which extremely heavy naval escorts with covering screens outnumbered the merchantmen under their protection and always there had been heavy losses.

Only three months before the Allied landings in North Africa the "Pedestal" convoy had been so severely battered from the air and from U-boat and E-boat attacks that out of fourteen cargo ships, only four had won through. Nine had been sunk and the Royal Navy lost an aircraft carrier, two cruisers and a destroyer. Malta, the George Cross Island, was effectively relieved by a supply convoy from Alexandria within weeks of Algeria coming under the Allies' control.

The main improvement in the situation since then was that the Allies were in a better position to counter attack the Axis air bases and to put up fighter patrols. Otherwise, even though the enemy was now very much on the defensive, the position had lost little of its danger for the likes of us, slow as we were and with an escort force stretched to its limits.

It was not without certain misgivings therefore that we approached that arena to the south of Sardinia where within twenty minutes of take-off the Luftwaffe or their Italian counterparts could give us their full attention. Giving Bougie a wide berth because of its unhealthy reputation for offshore surprises, we were approaching Philippeville when the next series of attacks started.

After more than a day and a half of scanning the skies and the sea for any trace of the enemy returning, the sound of the alarm bell almost came as a relief. In the dazzling mid-morning sunshine we saw the attackers approaching from ahead, flying low along our port side. Soon we were heavily engaged, as individual attacks developed wherever the enemy detected a weak spot among the streams of tracer.

The barrage was impressive and so was the daring and skill of the pilots who twisted and turned to avoid the heavier fire of the escorts and returned persistently, seeking a straight run to launch their torpedoes. It was not long before we saw a large cargo ship in the rear ranks enveloped in smoke, and heard the familiar sound of a torpedo blast.

By the time the flying visit was over the convoy was near enough to Philippeville for those ships due to leave it there to make their departure and, as we had done on previous occasions, they went with some alacrity. Within a few minutes another attack started. Whether or not it was a new wave or a return of the previous attackers was not clear.

Guessing that they knew as much about the pattern of convoy operations as we did by that time, I concluded it was the latter when the second attack was mainly concentrated on the small group of ships that were heading into port. With only their own guns and no support from the main escort they were obviously an easier target.

As we steamed beyond the eastern headland we thought we heard the sound of another torpedo exploding, but by that time most of the ships were out of sight. We were not neglected and the shooting match continued for some time, a distracting period when there was the strong inclination to look back at the stricken vessel in our wake, now seen to be settling with boats pulling away from her.

For the enemy she represented a victory indeed, having almost made it successfully through the Atlantic and the western Mediterranean to within a few miles of her unloading port. From the sight of her it seemed a foregone conclusion that her cargo of war stores, ammunition and military vehicles were destined for the bed of that wreck strewn sea.

The empty shell cases were by that time making as much racket as the Oerlikon fire and becoming dangerous underfoot. Magazines needed refilling and with so much to do it was not easy to keep any accurate tally on where one wave of attack ended and another began. The Bo'sun, whose quarters were near enough to the Marlin gun position for him to claim early possession, had also got through quite a lot of ammunition, but claimed he was only just getting into his stride.

We had seen no planes shot down and, though it would have been difficult to perceive what extent of damage they received, it did not seem possible that such daring as they demonstrated could have left them all unscathed. The attacks had been continuing for some time and it was now well into the afternoon and, apart from one ship definitely hit and another possibly sunk, the convoy had survived well.

An outburst of firing to seaward, where two of the escort ships seemed heavily engaged, brought the information from the third mate on the monkey island that E-boats were now involved. He had the advantage of the look-out's binoculars, but became too engrossed in the obscure conflict to give any coherent commentary.

Jacob Harteveld and I had set up the two redundant Lewis guns on the boatdeck. Their weak springs had been re-tensioned again and it seemed a good opportunity to try them once more to see how many rounds they would fire before jamming. It seemed that now we had entered E-boat territory anything with a low trajectory might prove useful. Fortunately the escort ships seemed to have taken care of the problem and I was not too unhappy to hear the cry from above the bridge that they had apparently been driven off.

Those Lewis guns which, intermittently, fired the same .303 ammunition as the Marlins were an irritation and a challenge, but I think both Jacob and I valued them secretly as a psychological prop.

Laid across a deck locker they were little more than defensive tokens, worn-out relics of Sergeant Bunce's first war, an ironic reminder of the elderly gunnery instructor who, after shaking his head over the Marlin, a modern American weapon, had spoken to me lovingly of the trusty Lewis. If he had been around I felt sure he would have made them bark more convincingly. Too many lesser experts had tried and perhaps that was the problem.

There was not much time for reflection, for soon the air attack on our section of the convoy claimed our full attention. The 12-pounder guns on some of the merchant ships in our vicinity were quickly back in action and streams of tracer followed as low flying planes dodged in and out of range. The P.O., who had taken over from Sergeant Bunce, had been holding his fire, but suddenly went into action with the port Oerlikon as a plane swerved in our direction.

It was holding its course, coming straight for us and provided him with a head-on target. It was still coming on when his gun jammed and even the scream of its engines could not drown his violent indictment of dud ammunition. The after gun and the Marlins were still firing and the gunner on the starboard wing of the bridge tried to bring his gun to bear.

Suddenly bits were flying off the bridge dodger, large chunks of canvas and woodwork, and the port shrouds and the rigging over the foredeck twanged in complaint. The plane, which by that time was swerving away under the concentrated fire of the ships near us, seemed miraculously undamaged.

Happily no-one on the bridge had been hurt and the damage done could easily be repaired. More serious was the destruction of some of the running rigging, particularly the severing of the topping lift on one of the derricks. Wire splicing had almost become an occupational therapy aboard *ODYSSEUS*, and that did not worry us, but it was a special quality of weight tested wire we would need to beg, borrow or steal.

The air attacks which had been going on since before noon until late in the afternoon were not resumed and as we steamed on towards Bone the Oerlikon gun was cleared of its damaged shell case and the magazine carefully inspected for any other rogue rounds. The P.O.'s indignation simmered on. He, not unnaturally, felt he had been robbed.

Entering port that evening was a taxing game of follow-my-leader, with each ship doing its best under the constant whip of the escorts not to run down the vessel immediately ahead as we filed through the long and veering swept channel. Standing by the flag locker to attend to the signal halliards I watched the second mate getting more and more testy as he tried to anticipate the awkward manoeuvres of the ship ahead whilst still keeping us out of the minefields on either hand.

Bone showed every evidence of the enemy's unflagging efforts over many months to put it out of action or severely disrupt its operational purpose. We passed the blackened hull of a burnt out tanker as we went in and saw another bombed hulk against a quay. Many buildings had gaping holes or were partly demolished, the rubble having been used to fill the craters all round the dock area.

It had the confident atmosphere of a port under siege where dogged defenders and triumphant blockade runners could congratulate each other in the sure knowledge that not many miles away, round the next main headland towards Cape Bon, their enemy counterparts were taking as much punishment and losing ground into the bargain.

The confirmation of what our opposite numbers on the Axis side were now undergoing came that morning with the comforting sight of two cruisers, several destroyers and a flotilla of motor torpedo boats flying the white ensign. We soon learnt that they were part of Force Q with a mission to intercept and destroy the enemy convoys sailing between Sicily and the ports of Bizerta and Tunis on which General Rommel now relied almost entirely for his supplies.

The first visitors we had were from a naval trawler. They came in search of potatoes which they claimed not to have seen in several weeks. We hadn't seen any in a long time and our compassion for their hard lot deepened immediately at their joy in accepting some tins of the dehydrated variety which our cook had never been able to transform into anything remotely edible.

We had some urgent scrounging of our own to do for, without a new topping lift, one of the derricks over our number two hatch was out of action. We did not have to look far. We were moored alongside a large, North American built standard ship, the *FORT*

HALKETT, operated by Denholm's of Glasgow. She was abundantly stored and her bo'sun was sympathetic to our plight.

He quickly located what we needed and soon we were passing a heavy coil of wire down to our foredeck. Working happily in the warm sunshine we quickly restored the situation and later played our gramophone to an appreciative audience of R.E. dockers, seamen from other ships, military police, cheerful Arabs and curious Frenchmen. It was a great success, especially the community singing, though we feared for the endurance of its replaced spring.

It was a disappointment to learn the next day that there was no free discharging berth, and we moved out to the mole and berthed stern-on next to the destroyer *LOYAL* whose launch generously included us in its regular liberty service to and from the shore.

It was through members of the destroyer's crew that we began to appreciate just how tough a time the enemy's supply ships were having. The *LOYAL* was taking a hand in it and we heard how, several weeks before whilst on patrol with another destroyer, her 4.7 inch guns had destroyed an enemy ammunition ship in an eruption of flame and steam.

One of the cruisers in port, *H.M.S. AURORA* the flagship of Force Q, had led an earlier attack with two other cruisers and two destroyers, in which a whole convoy had been annihilated. Their quarry of four supply ships and three escorting destroyers had been discovered in the approaches to Tunis and destroyed by gunfire in an horrific scene of burning escorts and exploding cargo carriers.

Whatever else we had to put up with we had never come under the attack of the still powerful Italian surface fleet. It was a thought which engendered some latent sympathy for those former brothers of the sea, the merchant seafarers Il Duce had committed to the wrong side.

Bone and Malta were the two strategic bases from which such convoys were being harried by surface patrols and submarines and it was no surprise to me to see Swordfish torpedo planes of the Fleet Air Arm approaching a nearby airfield. The enemy's shipping movements were also under constant threat from the mines laid across their path.

There was an air of cheerful gratification among those long since resigned to the dangerous occupation of the port. Over the few days we lay at the mole, or alongside the discharging berth, the enemy made no attempt to attack the place, a surprisingly long break much remarked upon. It was a bonus we had not expected and gave us the chance to indulge in social activities we had been generally denied.

We found a canteen among the battered buildings, run by an Army padre I think, and in the town itself a cinema where we joined a queue of navy and army personnel who took it with remarkable cheerfulness when it was later announced that the show was cancelled. Apparently the film had not arrived. We just hoped it was not lying on the bed of the sea somewhere off the coast.

As a substitute there was a French cinema showing a Hollywood production with local sub-titles. The Algerian audience chattered, applauded and sometimes argued with such enthusiasm the soundtrack was mainly inaudible. It was nonetheless entertaining.

The *PENSHURST*, which had sailed out with us from Port Talbot, was lying nearby and her crew presented us with some more pickles. We wondered at the enduring capacity of their steward's store and put some aside for Jim when he returned to us from hospital. I discovered that the mate of the ship was an old acquaintance and we exchanged promises that, whichever one of us should be the first home, he would pass on news to the other's family.

From a Norwegian ship, which we learned was expected to be released from the coastal supply fleet when she got back to Algiers or Oran, our fo'c'sle store received unexpected bounty. Our northern allies, well inured to the privations they would leave behind, presented us with several large cans of fruit cocktail easily identified as coming from some American military commissariat. How they had acquired them we did not ask, but gleefully carried them aboard.

CHAPTER TWELVE

Our voyage back to Oran was without incident and was marked only by the inspiring spectacle of the battleships *NELSON* and *RODNEY* and the aircraft carrier *FORMIDABLE* as we were nearing Algiers. They swept by with an escort of destroyers and provided us with a very convincing reason for the continued absence of the Italian capital ships and cruisers from our theatre of war.

As Force H, the powerful trio operated from Gibraltar and the naval base at Mers-el-Kebir near Oran. The only evidence of their local presence previously had been a Royal Marine band and well drilled naval contingent at the evening ceremony in the main square at Oran when the national flags of France, Britain and the Unites States were lowered for the night. It drew the largest crowd of Algerians we had seen assembled in that city and won much applause.

In the port there was the usual cargo awaiting us and we were told we were again bound for Bone. In the meantime there were one or two outstanding matters to be followed up with our masters ashore. Our mail had completely dried up. No-one had received any for several weeks and Albert, the cook's young assistant, had not had any word from his family in Cardiff for five months.

The Bo'sun, a determined man at the best of times and perhaps the most thoughtful observer of the crew's morale, was concerned that nothing had so far been done to replace certain ageing members of the ship's company who, in a properly ordered scheme of things, should not have been aboard at all. One in particular was an elderly resident of the firemen's fo'c'sle who, but for the war, would almost certainly not still have been at sea.

He was an old stager occasionally used as a spare hand down below, but whose main task was to keep those quarters clean and to collect the meals from the galley. The ship had long been his home, and he had never been heard to complain, but he was now clearly showing the strain. The Bo'sun, not for the first time, spoke to the Captain about it. It was fairly obvious that in a matter of weeks the North African campaign would be successfully concluded ashore and the time seemed appropriate.

If Captain Ruig had already made his own representations to those in charge of manning he never mentioned it, but that would not have been his style. He did not offer to do so now, but in his inscrutable way gave his blessing for the approach to be made by anyone else chosen to do so. As a result Jacob Harteveld, one of the Dutch greasers, and Joe Stoakes found themselves delegated to promote the suggestion at the Sea Transport office.

They were also asked to find out, if possible, why the ship's mail had not been delivered for so long. They were not long away.

They returned with some vague promises and no explanation of why our mail had dried up apart from the suggestion that it might have been lost at sea or misdirected to Egypt. The Bo'sun said something in his mother tongue which required no translation, but nobody else seemed at all surprised.

The previous autumn the ship's company had been speculating widely on what the future held for them and the ship in which their fortunes were circumscribed. Now the guessing game was restarting. Even though the operation into which the *ODYSSEUS* had been so precipitously thrust was approaching its victorious climax, the build up of war material, so obvious all round us, suggested further adventure.

It was a clue not difficult to follow as to intention, yet it left unanswered the question of where our hotch-potch fleet could expect to be taking its chances later that summer. About this time Eric and I fell in with some of the crew from the requisitioned tank transporter *EMPIRE DACE* who generously invited us aboard to join in their midday meal. It did wonders for our appetites though the table talk went only some way to satisfying our thirst for information.

The small ferry, originally built I think for some Turkish sea crossing, had proved so valuable an acquisition to the military supply line it now served it was almost certain that, so long as her luck held out, she would continue to be involved. Her crew thought so too.

It was a peculiar fact, but perhaps understandable that many members of the crew, indeed many of the people we met, were so involved in the exigencies presented by their own bit of the war its wider pattern had escaped attention. Suddenly it seemed the bits were falling more obviously into place and the picture becoming clearer. There was little doubt now that victory in North Africa would be the forerunner of a much wider thrust across the Mediterranean to continue the momentum on European soil.

The idea of a second front in southern Europe to drain the forces of an enemy increasingly hard pressed on the Russian front and with an impending threat to its Atlantic Wall, now seemed a logical move and the most likely one - even to the crew of the *ODYSSEUS* who had not seen a newspaper in nearly six months.

Meanwhile the final stages of the war in Tunisia thundered into their climax. There was an air raid alarm in Oran shortly before we sailed, but what followed was a desultory affair and it bothered us little. The enemy liked to keep an eye on shipping movements in order to plan its offshore operations and it was probably a reconnaissance attempt. We slipped out in the early morning much encouraged by the news that the trap was closing on Bizerta and Tunis, the enemy's last strongholds.

SHORE LEAVE PASS

The bearer *P. Quintin* Identity Card No.**X720/53/4**.

is a member of the crew of the *Odysseus*

and has permission to be ashore from 1300 hrs. until

1900 hrs on the following dates.

Date *2/3* Master's Signature

Date *1/4* Master's Signature

Date *3/4* Master's Signature

The bearer of this pass must be made to prove his identity. This pass is not valid unless it bears the stamp of the Naval Officer in Charge, Bone.

Outings ashore were strictly regulated.

If the enemy had intended to waylay our convoy, matters of greater importance must have kept them away, perhaps the protection of the Axis forces' own threatened lifeline between Sicily and Cape Bon now under much pressure. It came as no surprise to be ordered into Philippeville to await a free berth in Bone where, it was understood, the resolute air attacks had resumed soon after our departure.

We moored alongside an American Liberty ship on her first trip to a war zone and her crew were soon stepping aboard, firing questions, particularly about our scars, and generally demonstrating that spirit of enquiry and sociability so hard to resist. As it happened we were probably more curious about their ship, which was the first of those mass produced standard cargo carriers we had ever come near enough to properly inspect, though they had begun appearing in ever increasing numbers in Algiers Bay and at Oran.

They were America's answer to the Allies' mounting shipping losses and to that nation's immediate need to vastly expand its own merchant fleet following its entry into the war in December 1941. Built to a British design, that of a Sunderland shipyard, in pre-fabricated, all-welded sections, they were being assembled and launched in a matter of weeks and, in some cases, days.

It was an incredible feat of production, often performed by quickly trained workers of both sexes many of whom had never previously seen the sea let alone a ship. To meet such a remarkable propagation of steamers in convoy, all as alike as peas in a pod, was one of the heartening sights marking the change in the Allies' fortunes, something to set against the appalling losses still being inflicted.

They were not pretty or fast, but they carried a lot of cargo and a great deal of conviction. We had seen some with derricks bent like wisps of straw when put under their first strain, and had heard stories of others whose decks had split on their maiden voyages, but the searching tests of the sea were ruthless and such exceptions readily excusable in the face of the astonishing output.

Utility vessels they may have been but to the crew of the *ODYSSEUS*, whose culinary experience had long been a testimony to dietary deprivation, whose cramped quarters above the chain locker lacked so much as an electric fan, and whose personal hygiene depended much on a bucket with hot water drawn from the engineroom, the Liberty ship was a modern marvel.

It's iced water fountain, ample showers, well-ventilated accommodation amidships for all hands, refrigerated stocks of steak, spacious messrooms and seemingly inexhaustible supply of ice-cream, exposed to us an extension of sea life no ageing, German-built steamer could ever offer. Those of us who went aboard to reflect on such admirable arrangements bore up to it pretty well.

Our more serious frustration was to be reminded, apologetically enough, of what small store our American neighbours set upon an ample supply of tea. We had run out of it weeks before and, as most of them hailed from Boston, we hoped they could help us out, only to be reminded they never drank it.

There was disappointment too for one of our greasers, an experienced engineroom hand, who had at one time in his long career sailed in American ships. The chief engineer of the Liberty ship, who was obviously scouting for talent to improve his own team, offered the Dutchman a job which he was only too eager to accept. Not unnaturally Captain Ruig refused to release him and thereafter kept a careful eye on the rest of his crew.

Though we had still not received any more mail, some members of the crew got fairly recent news of events at home through other ships in that busy port. Eric met an acquaintance from Erith serving in the naval tug *NIMBLE*. Albert Bolton escaped from the galley long enough to meet some friends from Cardiff among the crew of the South American Saint Line's ship *ST CLEARS*. As he had not received any letters at all since we sailed from the Bristol Channel they had a lot to talk about.

The third radio officer of that ship who came aboard to see Jack Ridler turned out to be an old acquaintance of mine. As she would, with luck, be home long before any postal service could deliver our mail and certainly before we returned, hastily written letters for posting in Britain were gratefully handed over.

There was only one notable air attack in the few days we lay there. The barrage put up by the ships and shore defences, in which the gunners on the Liberty ship played an enthusiastic part, was as deafening as it was impressive.

When the last plane had headed for home and the smoke had cleared there was little sign of any damage and no ship had been hit. Philippeville, which had absorbed its fair share of punishment since the start of the campaign, looked much the same. Only the wreck of the *AURORA* gave any indication of the immense salvage task now getting underway to clear Algeria's battered harbours. She had been moved, to lie half sunken in shallower water, by the Royal Navy's ocean salvage ship *SALVENTURE* which had arrived from the eastern Mediterranean.

There was another isolated ship, moored at a remote buoy, to which our eyes were occasionally drawn over those few days. She was the small Norwegian steamer with whom we had previously sailed in nervous consort under the sole protection of a trawler some weeks before. The rumour was that there had been an outbreak of typhoid fever aboard. Some claimed it was a case of typhus.

A photograph from abaft-the-beam of the British cruiser AURORA, flagship of Force 'Q' operating from Bone against the Axis supply convoys - sister ship to PENELOPE, the ill-fated H.M.S. "Pepperpot".
(Courtesy of W.S.S.)

One morning her flag was at half-mast and later we heard that one of her British gunners was the victim of whatever contagious disease kept her in quarantine. It seemed to us particularly sad because we had learnt that after completing her long and dangerous stint she was due to be sent home because she was now too slow.

When the signal came for us to join the next convoy to Bone we sailed with an additional member of the crew, the well-fed cat from the Liberty ship. Through some perverse feline impulse it seemed she preferred our accommodation. It could hardly have been the cuisine.

However often she was returned she had quickly found her way back to the more humble abode the *ODYSSEUS* offered. In the end the Americans had bequeathed her to us and signed her off. Though Captain Ruig had not been consulted in the transaction and had shown no previous inclination to favour the cause of a ship's pet, he now indulged the animal lovers among us by accepting her adoption in the best spirit, as a vote of confidence in his own command.

This gentler side to the Captain's nature which we now glimpsed was reflected in other normally restrained members of our company who, in the superstitious way of seafarers, saw in the cat's strange preference some happy omen. Nonetheless those who knew more about cats and suspected, quite correctly as it happened, that our new arrival was soon to present the ship with her furry progeny, cautiously kept it to themselves.

As we negotiated the swept passage into Bone she purred contentedly in a sunny corner of the boatdeck and viewed with no apparent alarm an incidental tragedy that affected the rest of us more acutely. One of the outgoing escort ships shepherding the convoy whose berths we would fill, trespassed into the minefield and paid the price. The blast of the explosion near her stern brought her to an abrupt halt. Some survivors were being landed as we got in, but she was still afloat and I don't think she sank.

It came as something of a surprise to realise that Easter was already upon us and the urge to seek some spiritual replenishment, though not openly expressed except perhaps by Eric, stirred us to take our first opportunity of attending a non-denominational service. Jack Ridler found it for us, in the make shift canteen in the dock area where a throng of men from many units and all three services were already gathering and a portable harmonium was warming up with the voluntary.

We had no calender in the fo'c'sle and it came as something of a surprise to realise that, by coincidence, Easter Sunday fell on the anniversary of Anzac Day that year. Also by remarkable chance the Church of Scotland padre turned out to be a veteran of that grimly remembered carnage at Gallipoli on the Dardanelles in 1915. It set the tone for an address which held his long suffering congregation in rapt contemplation of their comparable good fortune.

It was more of an exercise in psychological rehabilitation than a sermon and it didn't take too long for the spare, greying figure in khaki to make us believe that any experiences of the past months had all been part of a proficiency test to help us face up to anything worse that the future might have in store. It certainly went down like a bomb.

If we had gone there in search of comfort or consolation we came away, as I am sure did most, with a sense of contrition for any whingeing of which we may have been guilty in the past, and a somewhat bolder sense of purpose. To my shame I never found out his name.

If such transient uplift brought a welcome boost to jaded spirits and a less critical acceptance of day-to-day tribulations, there was soon to be a solemn religious occasion in which the crew's underlying resentment would outweigh any comfort it offered. But in the meantime, with a rare break in normal duties, the crew of *ODYSSEUS* basked for a brief spell in the warm sunshine and relaxed.

Bone was the hub of various exciting endeavours and there was much to see. It would not have been surprising to find among the naval and military personnel many bomb-happy servicemen chafing at their extended exposure to the still frequent air attacks it attracted. Instead there seemed a pride of purpose about all that went on in that furthermost terminal of the Allied supply line, and with much justification.

Any day now they expected to hear that Bizerta or Tunis, or both had been taken by the First and Eighth Armies, yet the urgent activity of the port never flagged. The cargoes of war material kept coming ashore as ships holds were cleared and berths vacated to be quickly re-occupied by heavily laden arrivals. Some of it, obviously still urgently required, was reloaded into landing craft to be taken on to the small harbours of La Calle and Tabarka, the nearest discharging berths to the front line and the quickest route for delivering the rations.

Soon after first arriving in Algiers, La Calle had been mentioned to us as an intended coastal destination. Some of the men of the Royal Engineers Dock Units who had been there for a spell considered Bone a placid retreat by comparison and provided us with one more blessing to count. They cleared up for us another mystery. All the aviation and vehicle fuel we had seen delivered, and we had carried our fair share of it, had been in cans or drums. Yet we knew such a supply could never have been adequate.

We had never seen any tankers in coastal convoy and had not been surprised, in view of the perils, at their exclusion. Now we learned that two small tankers, the *EMPIRE BAIRD* and the *EMPIRE GAWAIN*, had been making the run to Bone regularly at night almost since the beginning. We had never sighted either though our courses may have run close in the darkness. It was a stimulus to hear of their continued survival.

An unusual aspect of Bone was the combination it achieved in such a constricted area of cargo port and operational naval base. Nowhere else I suspected would it have been possible to see an unpretentious steamer, with her derricks akimbo and her crew's washing strung out, lying alongside the flagship of a famous cruiser force, however briefly. Such things went unremarked and caused no hackles to rise in a port where every berth and every buoy usually had more than one urgent claimant.

On our earlier visit ratings aboard *H.M.S. AURORA*, flying the flag of Rear-Admiral C.H.J. Harcourt, took in our mooring ropes amid affable exchanges as we berthed temporarily in her shadow. They were as curious about our lifestyle as we were about theirs and complimented us on our rash of bomb-blight, still spectacular in spite of much painting. Whether it was meant as an acknowledgement of our good fortune or a reference to our high score of holes was not clear until one of them mentioned the name of *AURORA*'s equally famous sistership, *H.M.S. PENELOPE*.

The two cruisers had been in the Mediterranean since 1941 and, for a long time, involved in supporting the attempts to get supplies through to besieged Malta. It was whilst she was in dry dock for repairs to some bomb damage that *PENELOPE* came under constant air attack for eight days by waves of bombers bent on destroying the naval dockyard in Grand Harbour.

Her gun crews fought them off and she survived, but collected so many holes from near misses that she subsequently became known throughout the Mediterranean fleet as *H.M.S. PEPPERPOT*. It was a sobriquet of which her crew was proud, one that was used fondly by the men of the *AURORA*, and such oblique association through our own remarkable crop of holes gently fed our pride.

Though our own *AURORA* of the K.N.S.M.'s fleet now lay wrecked in Philippeville the classical connection between *ODYSSEUS* and *PENELOPE* was, relatively speaking, almost as close. In the mythological "Who's Who" she was our better half.

It was of passing interest, commented on by few and mainly by way of argument. The classicists in Amsterdam had somehow never got round to naming any one of their large fleet *PENELOPE*, but astonishingly had a *ULYSSES* to stake their fortunes twice in the hero of Troy. Such devious debate sidetracked a matter which might have been entirely forgotten but for an incident during our second sojourn in Bone which showed that someone else remained aware of the family connection.

The affinity we had found in Bone between all the services and between all ranks had much to do with the shared confinement of a constantly endangered community. It was no unusual experience to be greeted cheerfully by some stranger in uniform as if one was an enrolled member of that hard-pressed yet supremely confident fellowship.

It came as no surprise therefore to one of our gunners, a hostilities-only rating on watch at the gangway, when the august Captain of the *AURORA* paused on the quay one morning to cast an appraising eye over *ODYSSEUS*'s much disfigured appearance. After returning our shipmate's salute he delayed for a moment longer whatever urgent business he was upon and with amiable smile, succinctly observed: "The *S.S. Pepperpot* I presume."

For those members of the crew who had come to view their ship's role as that of a sacrificial workhorse, vitally employed, but with little expectation of the merest acknowledgement whatever her fate, recognition from so illustrious a quarter was an unexpected tonic. From being just an assigned convoy number or another furrow on a berthing master's brow, so simple yet generous an endorsement had elected *ODYSSEUS* to the club it seemed.

In the little spare time we had whilst the ship was discharging, Eric and I, sometimes with Sparks, stretched our legs in the not unpleasant country beyond the rubble and by chance came upon an ack-ack installation whose strange symmetry rivetted our attention. Set out in perfect geometric formation were sixty-four multiple rocket launchers, electronically connected for automatic, radar controlled firing.

If they were a surprise to us we imagined they would certainly have such an effect on the Luftwaffe and for the first time entertained some appetite for their next visit. We did not have long to wait. Returning to the port we witnessed the arrival in Bone of hundreds of German and Italian prisoners bound for the compounds where they would await shipment to the west.

The Italians looked relieved, smiling and almost happy. Their allies, as weary and dusty in defeat, bore themselves with gloomy defiance. Yet the war was not over for them.

That night the enemy returned with a vengeance and we realised what it meant to share the target area with a cruiser force at close hand. Their 4 inch high-angle guns had a tempo and noise range which drowned out the racket of all lesser armament except the pom-poms, which kept up their own deafening, yet highly inspiring, chorus. Waiting for the rockets was like waiting for the spectacular set piece in a fireworks display.

At a moment when it seemed from the throbbing of the engines above that a wave was circling to attack in turn, the rocket barrage roared into action with a sound that split the air like an express train entering a tunnel. High above us the box shaped eruption must have been devastating to any aircraft entering the trap. In fact, I believe three were brought down.

Bone had taken so much damage it was not easy, when dawn came, to see how much had been added, but the only damage we could detect among the shipping had come from the many shell fragments that gravity had returned to us, hot and sizzling. What the prisoners of war, who could not have been too far away, made of the perform-ance was anyone's guess.

In the sunshine of the following day Jacob Hartevelt and I had a stroke of luck. We met the crew of an airsea rescue launch who had a surplus of tea and happily handed it over to us with their best wishes.

We discovered our R.A.F. benefactors were getting their mail regularly, almost every week, and getting parcels from home as well. Though envious we were too polite to ask how they managed it, but realised they had some influence with quite an important airline.

On the day we were due to sail it was the birthday of Princess Juliana, heir to the Dutch throne. The *ODYSSEUS* flew four national flags with one at the bow and others at the trucks of her fore and main masts to supplement the ensign at her stern. As there were two other Dutch ships in the port which did likewise it made a striking display. The cook achieved his third memorable meal since Christmas and the crew were given a couple of hours off.

We had taken a passenger aboard, a Sergeant in the Royal Engineers in charge of a sectionalised steel pier which may have been originally intended for La Calle or Tabarka along the coast, but was being returned to Oran. He was to become a good shipmate once he recovered from the shock of realising that our regular bill of fare was somewhat less than nourishing.

133

Another new face aboard was that of a young and cheerful Algerian the Captain had signed on as a fireman. His ambition was to get to Britain and he took it in good part when he found he had to sleep on a bench in the fo'c'sle because there was no spare bunk. He turned out to be an industrious acquisition.

MEROPE (1,200 grt) - Built in 1918 she was the oldest of the K.N.S.M. fleet serving in the North African campaign. Ten members of her crew died and others were wounded when she was torpedoed and sunk off Cape Bengut, Algeria in April 1943.

(Courtesy of Nedlloyd)

CHAPTER THIRTEEN

There was sad news awaiting us at Algiers, tidings which were to disturb the crew of *ODYSSEUS* and for the first time to arouse an undercurrent of dissatisfaction and even anger with those responsible for arranging the movements of the coastal shuttle.

We were berthed alongside our old consort, the *PENSHURST*, in the naval section of the port among cruisers and destroyers and not far from the submarine depot ship *MAIDSTONE*. There was an unusually relaxed feeling in the air, almost an end-of-term atmosphere as the North African campaign entered what was to be its last week.

The sight of Jim van Ommeren on the quay, waiting to rejoin us brought immediate pleasure, but the grim expression on his normally cheerful face informed us at once that something of serious and almost certainly sorrowful import was about to be revealed.

He broke the news quietly, almost gently. The *MEROPE*, another of the company's small steamers even older than the *ODYSSEUS*, had been torpedoed five days before returning from Philippeville whilst we were in Bone. There had been heavy loss of life.

As Jim, who had been out of hospital for some days and had spoken with some of the survivors, named those who had died in the devastating blast, or quickly drowned in its aftermath, gloom spread through the ship. There were few aboard who did not know most of them well. In some instances they were close friends over the years, former shipmates, even neighbours at home in pre-war Holland.

Yet the grief was not confined to members of the Dutch crew, for one of those whose life had been so swiftly and drastically terminated was Jack Ridler's close friend, the wireless officer of the U-boat's virtually helpless victim. Sparks was quieter than I had ever known him. They had trained together, taken their certificates at the same time and had found themselves serving in close company in a campaign which, on land at least, was within days of its successful conclusion.

The *MEROPE* which had already taken its full share of risks up and down that grim coast with cargoes so volatile as to test to the uttermost the fortitude of any crew, had been sent from Philippeville in the company of only one other merchant ship under the escort of a minimally armed Royal Navy sloop.

In such water, patrolled hopefully and regularly by a ruthless enemy below and above the waves, so weak and slow a detachment could expect little chance of escape in any confrontation. In that sudden grief it seemed to the crew of *ODYSSEUS* that only the direst need in some crucial moment of the campaign could have excused the call for such a sacrifice.

It was an experience the crew of *ODYSSEUS* had faced back in March when our hopes for bad weather or poor visibility had fortuitously, or by divine intervention, been conveniently answered. Yet we had still felt as helplessly exposed as sacrificial lambs. Only the exigencies of that period, when aspects of the campaign in Tunisia hung in the balance, had detached our concern from any feeling of resentment.

If we had felt critical at all of those with the problems of organising our movements and weighing the odds against their success it lay in another direction. There were those aboard who felt our chances, if given the option, might have been better were we allowed under such circumstances to make our best speed sailing entirely alone. Now, when the details of the *MEROPE*'s loss emerged, even those who thought like that had to reconsider so unlikely a proposition.

She had sailed from Philippeville with the larger French steamer *CEVENNES* under the protection of the small sloop *ROTHE-SAY* whose heaviest armament, apart from her depth charges, was a 3 inch gun. Having safely reached Bougie, a notorious danger spot, the miniature convoy spent the night in the anchorage there before continuing its slow voyage to Algiers.

From our own experience we could imagine that in that predatory neighbourhood all those whose duties did not keep them below, or in the galley perhaps, would have been anxiously searching the sea and the sky for the first indication of any danger.

The three ships were heading west, well out to sea as their unseen enemy made the fateful sighting from inshore. At maximum range no-one glimpsed the U-boat's periscope and there was no warning ping on the escort's asdic. The salvo of torpedoes ran unseen with one inexorably on course to rip open the *MEROPE*'s hull with a blast so violent that few of those on or about her bridge would escape death or injury.

The shattering explosion instantly killed her master, Captain C.P. Decker, her mate and others including her radio officer. One of her British gunners named Cooper, injured in both legs, was blown over the side. As the sea poured into her the ship took a heavy list to port. There was no hope of launching either lifeboat, even if they had still been seaworthy, scarcely time even for her second mate to issue any orders as she settled in the water for her final plunge.

Within a minute the injured, helped by those who had escaped the blast, were following the wounded gunner into the sea with the real fear that the doomed *MEROPE*, which sank seconds later, would suck them into the vortex. Instead, as she disappeared, the swirling waters plucked from their lashings three of the liferafts which they had also had no time to launch and, soon after, littered the sea with pieces of timber, dunnage which had escaped from her ruptured holds.

The last man to escape was a British trimmer named Chadwick who had found himself trapped as the *MEROPE* went under, but was freed moments later and propelled to the surface. He grabbed hold of a smoke float, a buoyant canister, which was part of the flotsam.

As the second mate reached the temporary security of a damaged raft and checked on the comparative safety of the survivors drifting around he saw by his watch, which was still working, that only five minutes had passed since *MEROPE* had received her death blow. The *ROTHESAY* was, by now, searching vainly for the attacker determined at least to keep her down whilst the rescue of the remaining crew could be organised.

Bravely, Captain Le Gonidec Yves, master of the *CEVENNES*, ignoring any standing orders to the contrary, acted according to the more compelling tradition of the sea. Closing the scene of that sudden annihilation he slowed his ship's engines and quickly launched a boat to begin collecting the wounded from the pathetic debris. Soon the escort ship joined in and between them they rescued twenty-four men, several of whom were seriously wounded and in urgent need of hospital treatment. Nearly a third of the *MEROPE*'s company had been lost.

What the outcome might have been had the *MEROPE* been on her own was open to conjecture, but the gratitude of those plucked from the floating litter told its own story and those among the crew of *ODYSSEUS* who had previously advocated that choice took note. The gloom caused by the loss of so closely related a ship continued for several days and was shared by the crew of another of the company's ships, the *TITUS*, which was in Algiers at that time.

She had been engaged on the coastal supply route from early in the campaign and had the clearly visible evidence of her own close shaves with disaster. Only a few days after we had sailed west from Bone earlier in that month of April, whilst at anchor in the outer harbour of that port, her crew had experienced their narrowest escape in a particularly heavy air attack. She had been blasted by a near miss which burst less than a boat's length away from her foredeck.

The violence of the explosion had wreaked havoc to her bridge and chartroom and midships accommodation, blown out the hatchboards of her forward holds and caused extensive damage to her derricks, rigging, funnel and deck gear. Some fragments had cut through her starboard plates and carved their way out through the port side. Fortunately there was no damage below the water line and she had been able to get back to Algiers under her own steam.

When the Captain of the French ship arranged for a mass to be held in Algiers for those who had died in the sinking of the *MEROPE*, the service in their memory was attended by members of the crews of his own ship, the *ODYSSEUS* and the *TITUS* and those survivors not in hospital. Later the Captain of the *CEVENNES* was to drop a wreath over the position where the cruelly placid waters had so swiftly claimed her riven hull.

Such sombre diversion did not prevent the mate from devising new campaigns to keep us busy in port. He was helped to some extent by Captain Ruig's constant ambition to find the most convenient berth in that sprawling port. We moved three times whilst we were there and it was not without its consequences.

We first moved to a quay on which mounds of ore lay awaiting the day when the port would resume normal trading or the chance occasion when some of it could be shipped by a vessel returning to Britain. The *PENSHURST* was already there and we moored alongside. Her crew was jubilant because they had just heard she was bound for home.

Jim was happy for them and jovially suggested that the Sea Transport office must have realised that they were running short of pickles. But it was not so for, amazingly, they still had them aboard and were generous enough to supply our fo'c'sle with some more. As we watched our opposite numbers smartening up their ship for the return passage our envy must have been evident.

The mate of the *PENSHURST* had them oiling the steel decks. He was a man I had known previously at home and he laughed when I expressed the hope that our mate didn't get any ideas from him. I spoke too soon. Jim nudged me in the ribs and looking round I saw

139

our erste stuurman coming on deck. His face lit up immediately and his eyes shone with inspiration. The next morning we were hard at it with chipping hammers and scrapers preparing our own deck plates for an extensive treatment with a mixture of linseed oil and boot-topping.

It was a task interrupted only by the arrival of a lorry load of deck stores, supplies the Captain had ordered long before to serve the ship for another half year, gear that was well overdue. If they had been food stores our small deck crew might have tackled their porterage with more alacrity.

The labour involved was considerably increased because the delivery truck was stranded a long way down that baking quay, its passage blocked by a railway waggon which the mate would not let us move. Eventually, when we had transferred the bulk of the consignment and manhandled it aboard, some Algerians turned up to push the waggon out of the way.

All the while the mate watched over us assiduously with an air of gratification which suggested that such timely delivery of his long awaited gear had come as a bonus to his earlier inspiration. I think only Jim van Ommeren saw any humour in it. We moved berth again, soon afterwards, to a quay with closer access to the city, but found little opportunity of getting ashore.

Recreation was not a pursuit the crew had much opportunity to follow. Apart from stretching their legs ashore or sailing in some makeshift dinghy, rigged ingeniously by Jacob Harteveld, there was not much else on offer. There was no sports equipment aboard and any packs of cards which the ship possessed had long since become dogeared and grimy. Surprisingly, under the hot North African sun, the crew developed an enthusiasm for cricket.

It was, I think, the inspiration of our passenger, the congenial Royal Engineers Sergeant, still patiently waiting to deliver his portable steel pier to wherever it was bound. As the Algerian quaysides, broad as some of them were, were not designed for the wider game, the rules had to be rewritten which suited those Hollanders who had never known them.

They were also adapted to suit our basic, handcrafted equipment which mainly consisted of a bat shaped from a springy piece of dunnage board with spunyarn bound round the grip. The ball was, at first, a canvas contraption, packed with cotton waste and sewn up with sail-twine, but it proved much too light and too easily expendable.

140

A more satisfactory substitute was a monkey's fist, a particular piece of rope work used normally to weight the end of a heaving line, which could be more easily fashioned and which could be effectively ballasted with a pebble or steel nut packed inside. Even the most ferocious sloggers couldn't swipe them into the drink very often.

Most of the crew, including the third mate, and all the gunners became hooked on the eccentric pastime in which batsmen were quickly run out, often to the cheers of curious Arabs who stopped work to watch. The mate viewed such goings on with indulgent bewilderment and, more than once, I caught him shaking his head at what I think he must have seen as unseamanlike expenditure of valuable energy.

All the time we were in Algiers the advances on Bizerta and Tunis were nearing their inevitable conclusions and it was clear when the first of those bases fell on the 8th May that the end of the North African campaign was only a few days away. There was a sense of relief after so many months, but no renewed speculation on the prospect of the *ODYSSEUS* making an early voyage home. By that time most members of her crew had accepted the fact she would be staying in the Mediterranean.

It seemed an appropriate moment, and a convenient opportunity whilst we were in Algiers, to solve some of the problems which made our lives more irksome than they need have been. It was that forthright but benign intervener, the Bo'sun, who suggested it. He spoke for the engineroom crew as well and indeed could have been voicing the concern of the entire ship's company, particularly on the subject of our missing mail.

It was months since we had last received any letter and Albert Bolton, the young galley hand, had not heard from his family in Cardiff since we had sailed the previous year. The Dutch members of the crew, all voluntary exiles in the Allied cause, were missing the brief Red Cross messages which indicated whether or not all was still well with their kin.

Following the early stages of the urgently mounted operation to evict the enemy from North Africa many arrangements to help the morale of those in the three other services had been efficiently introduced. For some reason, perhaps the pressure of keeping ships such as *ODYSSEUS* busily engaged, the basic welfare of their crews did seem, if not entirely overlooked, to have been long neglected.

Once again it fell to Jack Ridler and me to table various suggestions made by the crew for a few elementary improvements through those agencies that existed ashore and who we hoped might be receptive. A resumption of our mail service was our top priority.

Tracking down the appropriate sympathetic ear was not easy. Aiming high we located the office of the Ministry of War Transport in a modern building in the Rue de Michelet where we were swiftly whisked aloft in a smooth lift hoping to see the man at the top. His secretary was charming and sympathetic, but he wasn't in.

Time was short and it was a disappointment. We had long since realised that communications ashore, in all but those matters of urgent priority, left much to be desired. However, more out of politeness than any wish to discuss our suggestions with anyone down the scale of command, we noted the name of an official with an office nearer the port, by the Quai Transatlantique.

As we had to pass it on the way back to the ship we decided to have another try, only to find our man engaged. Captain Ruig came in while we were there, on business of his own, and in his bluff style quickly claimed the attention which was his due. It seemed a ripe opportunity for him to promote the approach we were making on behalf of the crew, but he showed no inclination to introduce the subject, and was gone quickly with the barest of acknowledgements.

We then met an official who was, I think, in charge of the manning pool from which crew replacements were supplied to cover injuries, sickness or fatalities in the coastal supply fleet. It was also intended to supply reliefs for crew members wishing to take a few days ashore between trips, an idea, we were told, suggested by Admiral Cunningham as a break from the arduous shuttle.

Apparently there had not been many applicants and we guessed why. It was not an idea which would have appealed to the crew of the *ODYSSEUS*. Spartan as conditions were in her confined and over-crowded accommodation, unappetising and deficient her culinary scale, unremitting, laborious and nerve-testing her involvement, she was still the nearest thing to home.

Being put ashore even for an officially sponsored jaunt would seem almost as bad as being marooned on some inhospitable strand. There would also be the deep suspicion that when the break was over they would find themselves in some other ship far removed from their close friends. The crew of the *ODYSSEUS* had long since become a family whom discomfort and danger had drawn together even more closely.

It might otherwise have puzzled us why the head of the family had never passed on the proposal, for our Captain must surely have known about it. It was not altogether an unworthy thought that the least risk of losing any members of such a well-knit team would have been anathema to him and reticence came naturally to Captain Ruig.

Clearly the well-meant idea had not taken off and the man who seemed to be in charge of it was ready to admit that the welfare of those engaged throughout the campaign in running supplies had been overlooked from the beginning. It was good to know that somebody, an august being at that, had eventually drawn attention to it and it seemed ungrateful to turn down the offer, though we promised to pass it on.

In return he promised to do what he could about our mail, but we came away without much hope of any sudden boost to our morale in that quarter. When we told the Bo'sun of our lack of success he was disappointed but showed no surprise. Sailors inherit a traditional cynicism, especially in wartime, for those who command desks.

When we passed on the proposal for anyone who felt that a rest ashore might do them good to apply, the response was as unenthusiastic as we expected. Indeed Jacob Ouwehand, the only man in the fo'c'sle with a sufficient wardrobe to dignify such a sartorial challenge, seemed quite nervous in case it was made compulsory.

Joe Stoakes considered the opportunity from a different aspect, but quickly concluded that any brew available in Algiers could in no way compensate for the pints he occasionally enjoyed as a guest of those Sergeants' messes temporarily established by dock units in the ports down the coast. To the best of my memory the matter was never discussed again.

Our delay in Algiers was explained about that time when the ship had a visit from a surveyor. Insurance regulations and their periodic cover required a shipmaster's attention even in the circumstances of her wartime engagement. Captain Ruig was, no doubt, making sure that all her certificates were in order and up-to-date. It was a factor which was soon to spare the ship's company the embarrassment of a confrontation with the Sea Transport officials.

It had an innocuous beginning one hot afternoon when we failed to join a convoy bound for Oran. On such a day the cool sea breeze would have been welcome, but the crew was not too disappointed.

Some of them were in fact relieved because Jack Ridler, who had doggedly arranged a last-minute appointment with a key official of the Ministry of War Transport in town, had gone ashore to present our modest suggestions for improving morale and was late returning.

I don't suppose the Captain would have sailed without his radio officer, but he was also adrift until the last minute. He swept aboard with Jack, hot and dusty, close on his heels. Then, without any explanation, he tersely ordered those moorings which had already been taken in to be replaced and left the mate and the Bo'sun to announce that we would not be sailing until the next morning at 4.00am.

Such changes in schedule were not unusual and caused little comment until some time later when the crew discovered that the *ODYSSEUS* and the homeward bound *PENSHURST* would be sailing in consort with a single escort. Nobody was happy about that. The fate of the *MEROPE* was still fresh in everyone's mind and, among those who saw her loss and that of so many of her crew as a needless sacrifice, the rancour would long simmer.

The urgency which had dictated all our movements over previous months seemed temporarily to have gone out of the operation. It was almost certain to return, but at that moment it appeared to the crew that whatever cargo awaited us at Oran could not be so desperately required anywhere as to justify so casually presented and unnecessary a risk.

In the critical months such occasional renunciation of the strong convoy system as there had been had always seemed a questionable gamble, dictated only by dire emergency. Now, to the crew of *ODYSSEUS*, it seemed that someone ashore was labouring under the delusion that the enemy at sea had been as thoroughly routed as the enemy on land which was certainly not the case.

Yet orders were orders, but if the Captain had any intention of challenging them he was, not unnaturally for him, keeping it to himself. Whether he was aware of the general reaction or not he gave no indication of it and shortly afterwards went ashore, and we guessed he would not be back until late.

Because most of the discussion in the ship was in Dutch the events which followed came as a surprise though it was not difficult to sense the unusual tension. Again it was our normally placid Bo'sun who stepped in to speak for his compatriots, indeed for the whole ship's company excluding the gunners, whose usual detachment in such domestic dramas was accepted as being above reproach.

Also watching events with fascinated neutrality was our passenger, the Royal Engineers Sergeant, who had sensed the mounting drama and, no doubt, awaited its outcome with some interest. Though he had no idea where his patent pier would eventually be bound he was still anxious to move it along.

Before the night watches were set the Bo'sun, every bit as grimly determined as he had always been to claim our Marlin guns as his own, told Joe Stoakes, Eric and me that it had been decided by the mates, the engineers and the other members of the Dutch crew to confront the Captain when he returned. Whatever he had in mind as head of the family he was going to have to listen to their protest and the Bo'sun was going to do the talking.

He left instruction for whoever was on watch not to leave the gangway and to call him the moment the Captain appeared and then to rouse all hands. It had all the elements of a volcano about to erupt, an issue of seething family dissatisfaction rapidly approaching the boil. In the event no-one, even those not directly involved, required to be awakened.

By the time the Captain returned at midnight the ship's company was already stirring and as soon as he had reached the saloon most of his officers and crew were ready to join him. If it came as a surprise Captain Ruig showed no signs of it though the expressions on the faces of the three guests he had invited back for a nightcap ranged from astonishment to mild alarm.

Much of what passed was in Dutch and most of the speaking was done by the Bo'sun supported by nods of approval from those whose strong views he represented. Those who couldn't follow guessed he was laying it on strongly against the Sea Transport planners. It did not take long and seemed to end in deadlock with the Captain insisting that we would still sail at 4.00am.

Though the matter had obviously not been resolved by the time the crew had withdrawn, the Bo'sun seemed quite philosophical again, almost cheerful in fact. When he told us the watchman would not be turning us out at dawn I had the feeling his thoughts were not dwelling on open mutiny. I got the impression that he knew the working of the Captain's mind better than any of us.

Jim van Ommeren who translated much of what passed for the benefit of the non-Dutch speakers had been much taken by the bulging eyes of one of the Captain's astonished guests. In the saloon he had been busy nudging me to note the man's goggling expression and before turning in again he practised it once or twice to add to his repertoire. It relieved the tension in the fo'c'sle.

It was broad daylight when the Bo'sun called us. The *ODYSSEUS* had not moved and he was still all smiles. It seemed the Captain had changed his mind and though he did not know on what official pretext we were sure he had a good idea. It seemed we would be sailing in a proper convoy in a day or two's time.

The atmosphere had changed completely in those few hours. Everyone seemed more cheerful and not merely because our sailing had been postponed. There was certain elation among the protestors who believed that the crew's attitude had prevailed or, at least, been satisfactorily acknowledged.

No-one gloated and the Captain was not heard to refer to it again. Officially, it was understood, he had declined to sail because of a delay in the production of some document or other associated with the surveyor's inspection. It was an ace he had been holding up his sleeve all the time, we did not doubt, and honour was satisfied all round it seemed, but if anyone had won the day I felt pretty sure it was the Bo'sun.

The mate was in a particularly cheerful mood and failed to notice how many shore passes were signed later that day on behalf of his department. Such neglect enabled me and Eric to accompany Jack Ridler on a rare cultural expedition which, if it soothed our spirits, caused our chief officer more than a little anxiety.

Algiers had acquired several amenities to attract us beyond the waterfront and for an all too brief interlude we escaped to enjoy Walt Disney's "Fantasia", showing at the comfortable air-cooled cinema near the Alletti Hotel. We wished we had persuaded Jim to go with us for the sight of cartoon elephants performing ballet would have specially entranced him.

Afterwards, watching the sun go down from a serene hillside beyond that spectacular city, we took silent stock of a phase of the war now in its last hours and, walking back down ancient streets, contemplated the next phase everyone sensed was soon to open. It was Sparks who wondered where the *ODYSSEUS* would be when Christmas came round again.

There was a shock awaiting us when we saw she was missing from her berth, and a feeling of relief when we discovered her moored not far away. The mate was looking hot and not as avuncular as when we had last seen him. He had had to move her to another quay mainly with the assistance of the gunners who, no doubt, performed with enthusiasm, but he was not pleased.

Passing on a good turn, Eric and I the next day assisted the crews of two landing craft newly arrived on the coast to moor more snugly in their allotted berths and got the news that Bizerta and Tunis had both fallen. It was heartening intelligence whose effect was only marginally surpassed by the satisfying discovery that one of the Royal Navy vessels possessed a considerable store of tea in sealed tins, and that her youthful R.N.V.R. skipper was happy to part with some.

On the day we left to join a regulation convoy bound for Oran there came the news that all enemy resistance in North Africa had ceased, but if Algiers had hoped for any long breathing spell there was to be disappointment.

Within hours of our departure there was an air attack on that port which demonstrated the ability and determination of the Luftwaffe to keep up its offensive. Sadly, we were to learn later, their sole victim was the small British coaster *DORSET COAST* which was sunk in her berth. Only a few days before she had managed to extricate herself from a dangerous situation when a Norwegian ship alongside had caught fire and the flames had threatened to spread.

Though our trip to Oran could not have been more peaceful, apart from the usual depth charge alarms, there could be no doubt that it would be a long time yet before the enemy's widespread strikcs against shipping would in any way relent. The chances were that in the next stage of operations they might even be stepped up.

CHAPTER FOURTEEN

The cost of victory in North Africa had been high and the responsibilities that came with it were suddenly evident. Every day we lay loading in Oran we watched a seemingly endless stream of Axis prisoners filing disconsolately ashore from the merchant ships and other transports arriving from the ports nearest to the scene of their overwhelming defeat.

All around them the vigorous build-up of stores and equipment flowing in from Britain and North American continued apace - a sure indication that the Allies would not pause long before their war machine rolled forward again. It must have been a shock to the unshaven, weary-eyed men to gaze on such abundance of material and so many ships all committed to the downfall of Fascist Italy and the German Fatherland.

As we had already witnessed in Bone, the Italians were less demoralised, more relaxed, many clearly happy that for them the war was over. The Germans, who had fought so bitterly with their backs to the sea, bore themselves with an air of defiance which explained unequivocally why the campaign had lasted so long. For them one felt the war was not over.

They formed up like men still under command, glad to be stretching their legs after so long and arduous a journey, and mostly they sang as they were marched off to whatever temporary compound awaited them.

For the first time I heard German voices singing "Lili Marlene", surely the most haunting of Second World War songs. Its effect was theatrical in the most memorable sense as it gradually faded into the distance where several hundred men marched into captivity under the setting sun. Even those members of the Dutch crew with the bitterest memories of the occupation of their motherland listened silently to that poignant expression of forlorn hope.

There had been no "Dunkirk" for them, no reversal even of the roles played in the evacuations of Greece and Crete, so costly in British naval and merchant ships two years before. The Royal Navy and the Allied air forces had seen to that. One thing it brought home to us was the fact that on our next trip down the coast we could expect plenty of company aboard for the return passage.

We felt sure now that we would be heading for Bizerta and there was a new excitement in the air. To reach Cape Bon would be breaking new ground. Significantly it established an open route at last to Malta and the Eastern Mediterranean, though it would not be without its surprises and lingering dangers.

The fact the *ODYSSEUS* would be steaming now into waters in which Homer's hero and his followers had once been compelled to linger was a satisfying contemplation to me, but to most of our crew the inspiration I think was the merest thought of any change of scenery.

By that time we had come to know almost every cape and headland along almost 500 miles of coastline and the sudden promise of seeing beyond that farthest promontory appealed to all. Some members of the crew had known Bizerta and Tunis in better days and they alone held any reservations over what we could expect.

Before we left we unloaded our passenger's sectional pier and said goodbye to the Royal Engineers Sergeant. It was intended that he should demonstrate its use and its assembly to units of the American army in preparation for the major operation which was clearly being planned. We were sorry to lose him and in some ways, I think, he was sorry to go.

Before leaving us he made a generous gesture by tracking down an ice-cream machine aboard a neighbouring American ship and returning with two or three pails of that cooling commodity. I think he had meant to get beer, but under the Stars and Stripes most ships were dry. His farewell contribution was a great success and in the fo'c'sle it was no surprise to see Jim van Ommeren shovelling it down with huge delight.

We sailed with a cargo of ammunition, a consignment of American army rations and many drums of special oil for defensive smoke screens. It was a large convoy, strongly escorted and attracted no enemy interference, yet was not without its alarms. At one stage, beyond Algiers, on lookout duty at night I picked out the rapidly approaching trails of what I immediately took to be two torpedoes speeding towards us.

Their unwavering courses rapidly converging on our heavily laden hull somewhere below our bridge, brought an urgent cry to my lips, though I imagine it would have been too late. In spite of the cold night air I could feel the sweat on my palms as, unexpectedly, the parallel phosphorescent tracks swerved away to seaward and I recognised two dolphins in pursuit of smaller prey.

We were kept on the alert also during the day following a message from the commodore ship to expect an important signal, which eventually came as we were nearing Bone. The coastal waters beyond, and particularly the approaches to, Bizerta were obviously still being swept for mines although a preliminary passage had already been cleared.

The minesweeping operation in the waters around Cape Bon must have been immense as the defences laid by the enemy stretched for miles in all directions to protect the approaches of their own supply ships to Bizerta and Tunis. In addition, a great many Allied mines had been laid over previous months in an attempt to disrupt Axis sea traffic.

It was no surprise therefore when we were ordered to anchor outside Bone which had now become a waiting area for ships proceeding further. Sprightly motor torpedo boats were busy shepherding the flock into local bays and warning them to be on the alert for air attacks which had been stepped up since the end of hostilities to the east.

Apart from being roused during the night to change anchorages we were left in peace and the next morning found the ship lying off a sunny beach which had all the appearance of a holiday lido. As convoys of military vehicles trundled past on the shore road the catcalls of the semi-naked warriors relaxing by the sea echoed across the bay and made us wonder why we had never found such a basking ground.

Captain Ruig was sick and it was the mate wearing his best uniform who went ashore to attend the convoy conference. He returned before long with dire tales of what we could expect round the corner, mainly gleaned from the master of another Dutch ship, the *MAAS*, I think. He had just got back from Bizerta and warned of frequent air attacks and the danger from E-boats, still operating from Pantellaria, the Italian island to the east of Cape Bon. There was still no mail.

We weighed anchor that afternoon and formed up in a small convoy made up of cargo ships of modest draught and salvage ships whose onward journey was of even greater importance we would soon discover. By nightfall the tension was back and became noticeable again at dawn, but there was still no sign of the enemy and soon we got our orders to anchor in a bay near Bizerta with two Norwegians and one British ship. The others sailed on bound for Tunis or the George Cross island of Malta.

The first Allied ships to get through had discharged their cargoes into landing craft outside the port whose entrance, we had been told, had been severely blocked.

It was not quite true by the time we made the attempt the following day, but on the whole was no exaggeration. Before the Allied first Army arrived the defenders had gone to great lengths to put the port out of action. The French pilot who came out to us told of twenty-six wrecks, most of which had been deliberately scuttled, some on top of each other.

I was at the wheel as we went in and gathered from him that there had been little time to move much of the vast obstruction which would need explosive demolition in due course. But he seemed optimistic, having already taken some shallow draught naval craft and at least one small cargo ship part of the way up the long gullet which led to the main naval port at Ferryville.

It was a tortuous operation. Whichever way we swung there seemed to be a wreck blocking our passage, some on their sides and others with only their masts showing, but it was the completely submerged ones which were the problem. Captain Ruig, who had by now recovered and was understandably anxious not to imperil his ship needlessly, issued sudden orders, sometimes in Dutch, and I was not unhappy when Jacob Harteveld eventually relieved me.

Even berthing her caused its problems, because of the obstructions in the water alongside the shore. The first attempt almost grounded us on some deep lying obstacles, but eventually we found a clear stretch where we could make fast and prepare to discharge.

The scene all round us was one of utter devastation, much of it undoubtedly caused by an enemy bent on wreaking the maximum of havoc as its time ran out. It was difficult to tell where such efforts began and where the destruction by Allied bombs and shells had ended. As far as the eye could see both sides had, between them, reduced much of the area to rubble.

The litter of abandoned equipment, weapons, vehicles and wrecked aircraft, some still smouldering, lay on every hand. Short of a major earthquake and, perhaps, a tidal wave only the visitation of modern war could have left so desolate a landscape in its train. Whether or nor it had ever been part of the land where Homer's Lotus

Eaters had led their idyllic existence, recent events had left no clue. If any trees of any kind had ever grown there the evidence had gone.

In the uncanny silence the voices of the few servicemen we could see sounded unnaturally loud. But a group of Americans, soldiers of a dock unit, some of whom we recognised from Oran, were waiting for us and soon the crashing of our hatch boards coming out and the drumming of the ship's cargo winches was restoring the beat of life to a port whose strategic importance would ensure its eventual resurrection.

Even without the sophisticated gear with which they had handled our cargoes in Oran, the G.I.s from such inland states as Kansas and Kentucky pitched in with a will and we knew we were not going to be there long.

It was a Sunday and later in the day we were able to wander ashore amidst that debris of defeat, ever careful of booby traps, but with a widening curiosity about the final stages of a resistance which must have been ferocious. Skirting the water side we made towards what had been a town, but now had all the appearance of a demolition site with few buildings entirely intact.

The litter of personal possessions strewn haphazardly in the forecourts of wrecked villas told the tale of hasty abandonment and subsequent scavenging by those small groups of Arabs who had moved in from the wide countryside and could now be seen encamped nearby. Jack Ridler found a church which seemed undamaged until we moved closer and saw the bomb crater alongside and the gaping holes in its walls and roof.

Its stained glass lying in fragments caught the sunshine and some shrubs, half buried at the entrance, were in vivid flower. Beyond the sunlit altar with its vase of withered blooms was a doorway through which we could see an embroidered cloth covering a coffin resting on a table. If we had been searching for signs of life the drama of an abandoned funeral service seemed to provide us with the sombre answer.

Indeed we were to catch a glimpse of only four of Bizerta's citizens, hovering silently like lost souls among the rubble of their razed homes. Soon Eric and I and the others, turned our attention to the wide array of martial impedimenta lying where it had been abandoned or destroyed.

There were many more servicemen encamped around us than we had at first supposed, including the crews of several Bofors guns we were happy to note. Without them our air defence would have been very thin. We found stray parties of British soldiers collecting up the arms surrendered, or just dumped, by the Germans and Italians. We were invited to inspect a store where an armourer with all the pride of an exhibition curator showed us an amazing range of automatic weapons and rifles stacked neatly in catalogue order.

His particular enthusiasm was for a collection of heavy calibre German machine guns which he much admired. He also showed us the evidence of an underground contribution to the Allied cause - an entire case of dud ammunition of Czechoslovakian origin.

In the presence of such war surplus the idea quickly came to mind of trading in our two ancient Lewis guns for something more up-market, but it was an approach he quickly scotched. All his hoard had been accounted for, but he hinted that among the considerable array of weaponry still lying around we might yet find what we were looking for, reminding us not to forget the ammunition.

In the few days remaining such purposeful inspiration took us further afield. We did not find what we were looking for, but across the water where there was some evidence of a last ditch battle we collected several Italian Carbines which were to provide much diversion at sea, shooting at bottles.

Our unrestricted wanderings took us to the perimeter of an airfield where we found many German fighter planes and a large number of other aircraft deliberately wrecked by the enemy. Piled in heaps, partly burnt with broken wings, distorted propellers and dismembered undercarriages, they made an awesome sight. There were float planes of French origin on a nearby slipway also damaged and burnt.

The airfield on which lay many more wrecked aircraft had been pattern bombed with such accuracy the craters seemed geometrically spaced. In German dugouts trophies of all kinds lay around, from German helmets, bayonets and ammunition pouches to unopened packets of field rations. Some of the latter contained packets of instant porridge which, when mixed with water, looked as uninviting as anything which came from our own galley.

It was in such a dugout that one of us found a German newspaper of recent date whose main front page headline immediately caught my eye. There in large print was the name of the ill-fated British submarine *THETIS*, the victim of a pre-war sea tragedy which had riveted world attention in 1939.

It was the first daily newspaper any of us had seen in seven months and why it should have resurrected that particular story was a mystery until Jacob Harteveld translated it. As he read it out it became even more compelling.

All that most people would have remembered about the *THETIS* was her loss four years before and the agonizing wait as desperate efforts were made to rescue those ninety-nine men, including many shipyard workers, who were doomed to die. For the first time, we learnt from that German news sheet that the submarine which had failed to surface from her first trial dive in Liverpool Bay had been salvaged and, since 1940, had been operating successfully against the enemy as *H.M.S. THUNDERBOLT*.

The tragic sequel, which was the purport of the broad headline, was the news that she had been sunk finally by an Italian escort ship whilst attacking a convoy a few weeks before off the coast of Sicily. Triumphant as the announcement was there was yet a touch of homage in its presentation for her lost crew. It was a strange way to learn something more of the war around us and Jim van Ommeren who was always affected by sad things solemnly folded the page and put it in his locker.

It was hot in Bizerta and we were plagued by mosquitoes. The fo'c'sle became untenable at night and most of the crew chose to sleep on deck. Either way we would have been eaten alive had not someone discovered some mosquito netting among those depressing acres of discarded equipment. Soon everyone was hunting for it, our first real bonus of the Allied success.

Beyond the devastation we found the country scenic if not entirely picturesque and stretched our legs, though we envied those, mainly French naval types, who had already staked their claim to numerous German motor cycles and scout cars. The ship's company had earlier set its corporate eye on an apparently new vehicle of that type which one of us had discovered not too far away still packed in its crate.

The intention had been to swing it on deck before we left and we had pleasant visions of seeing much more of the interior wherever future voyages took us. We kept a close eye on it, but it disappeared one night and undoubtedly found its way over the ramp of one of the naval landing craft berthed further up the channel. Some of the crew managed to get to Ferryville where at least one estaminet still operated and Jacob Harteveld reported favourably on it.

When our cargo was almost discharged we were told to prepare those holds already cleared for taking in 500 prisoners-of-war, a thought provoking task. The ventilation below the tweendecks was poor indeed and the reek of mixed cargoes, particularly aviation fuel, was bad enough when the holds were empty. With so many bodies closely confined it would be almost overpowering.

Fortunately that problem was postponed by the arrival of two American landing ships more suitably equipped for such a purpose. But it was only a task delayed because many more prisoners were now at Bone, where they had been conveyed overland, and our orders were to call there when we left. It gave time however, to contemplate the prospect of not only coping with those in confinement, but of having to accommodate a large number of guards in a ship in which living space was already severely strained.

Gunners Dave Bowdley (arms folded) and James Johnston ashore in Oran.

Before we left, one of the navy's Sea Transport officers hurried aboard to deliver mail and the news echoed round the ship to everyone's delight. When he explained that he had only one letter, for one of the gunners, the disappointment was intense. It was nothing to the disillusionment of the surprised gunner. His joy turned quickly to dismay when he read the contents only to discover that the girl to whom he thought he was engaged had broken it off to marry someone else.

The general astonishment which greeted the first letter to arrive aboard after so many anxious months turned to instant resentment when the irony became clear. How the Fleet Mail Office had managed to reach us at last in so outlandish a haven was a mystery and the S.T.O. man, sensing his unpopularity as the messenger, slipped quickly ashore without explaining it.

As the *ODYSSEUS*, now drawing much less water in her light state, made her way to the sea and towards the cool breezes of the bay, the noise of blasting nearer the entrance confirmed that Bizerta was in the process of getting back into full operation. Explosives were being used to carve a much deeper channel through the jam of scuttled ships.

The urgent work paused only for us to squeeze our way out and to anchor beyond the mosquito zone where we were ordered to await the arrival of a ship which had unloaded at La Goulette near Tunis. She was the *EMPIRE TERN*, a steamer recruited from the Great Lakes I believe, one of the ships which had recently arrived in the Mediterranean to relieve some of those which had served throughout the campaign. She looked even older than the *ODYSSEUS* and profoundly demonstrated Britain's shortage of such small ships through its frightful war losses.

The American landing craft with their human cargoes had followed us out and sailed ahead of us. We followed more slowly, in separate formation, with one escort ship. Whilst we had been at Bizerta the air attacks we had been warned of had failed to materialise. Only one enemy plane had been heard, presumably making a reconnaissance. Now, as we hauled away, the sound of attacking formations filled the night air with its sinister beat.

In the distance we saw the tracers streaming up and wondered what the raiders hoped to add to the battered remains of that ravaged seaport.

If they had been seeking a likely target we guessed some of them had found it when we heard planes flying towards us, probably attracted by our phosphorescent wake and bow waves. As they roared over at, no great height, the temptation to open fire was strong indeed but, by some prior agreement I think, the gunners on all three ships resisted the urge. To our relief the planes ignored us and soon, from well ahead where the landing craft were making their own way, we saw arcs of tracers hosepiping the night sky.

Their fire quickly died away as the enemy, apparently snubbing them as well, swung back towards the land as if realising that any blows they struck at sea might mean certain death to helpless men of their own side. We hoped we were right in that conclusion because our main concern at the thought of being used as a transport for war prisoners was a horrifying vision of disaster striking with such scant hope for those battened below.

The only other alarm that night was mainly of personal concern, although I am certain it scared the mate as much as it did me. It was in the last minutes of my watch at the wheel, approaching midnight. I suddenly felt my knees buckling and keeled over without warning. The mate, who was on the starboard wing of the bridge, apparently heard and noticed nothing for my collapse had been so quick, without any dragging clutch at the helm, that the trusty *ODYSSEUS* with her well balanced rudder held a steady course.

Fortunately he stepped into the wheelhouse moments later to go to the chart table and found me in some shock slumped on the grating. His reaction, as he helped me to my feet, was a stimulus of sorts for it was clear his concern for me was having a struggle with his navigational priority. I guessed his eyes were popping for the light was dim, but could easily detect the pitch of astonishment in his rapid Dutch.

Happily it was eight bells and Jim, who was on the middle watch, arrived to relieve me. Instinctively I gave him the course and, though still startled by the turn of events, noted with some satisfaction that the ship was still on that heading. Apart from the lingering aches and pains which occasionally recurred following my crash-landing in the after well-deck, I had not been aware of any cautionary physiological symptoms. I had no doubt that the mate would be consulting the ships medical guide, but I took Jim's advice and turned in.

CHAPTER FIFTEEN

Soon after we had safely arrived in Bone and berthed alongside the *EMPIRE TERN* the mate was again consulting his medical book, this time in an attempt to identify a mysterious infection which had begun to lay low other members of the crew. Its symptoms seemed to be giddiness, stomach pains and general weakness and, hazarding a guess, it was due to the water with which we had topped up our tanks in Bizerta.

After a few hours sleep I felt quite well and had put down my own startling experience to overstraining my injured back and to the fact that the heat and mosquitoes had made any real sleep difficult whilst we had been at that port. Now it seemed we had the beginning of an epidemic aboard. The third mate, I think, was the first to go down with it, but Eric was also feeling unwell and one of the firemen and other members of the engineroom staff were affected.

It was a problem which was soon temporarily forgotten when the enemy decided to remind Bone that it had not been reprieved. That night, just as I was about to turn in, there was the sudden whine of an aircraft beginning its dive and as it developed into a shriek the alarm bell sounded. It was still ringing when the first stick of bombs exploded along the quay, and too close for comfort.

There were only a few short bursts of fire as the attacker roared off and it seemed that for once the early warning radar had been beaten. By the time the next plane came screaming in the reception committee was properly organised and with many ships, including cruisers, in port that night erupted with a barrage almost more nerve-racking than the crash of bursting bombs.

It seemed a particularly desperate attack, and every plane crew which survived that hellish response must have felt fortunate indeed. In the half-hour it lasted hot fragments of the bursting missiles came down like hail at times, hissing as they hit the water and pinging and clanging on steel decks. At one stage during the raid, the *ODYSSEUS* had its own drama when the cartridge casing of an Oerlikon round split, leaking powder which caught fire and endangered a magazine.

The petty officer cleared the bridge as he tackled the problem and it was some time before his gun was back in action. When it was all over nothing afloat seemed to have been hit and the next day Jack Ridler, who had been ashore in an unsuccessful search for our mail,

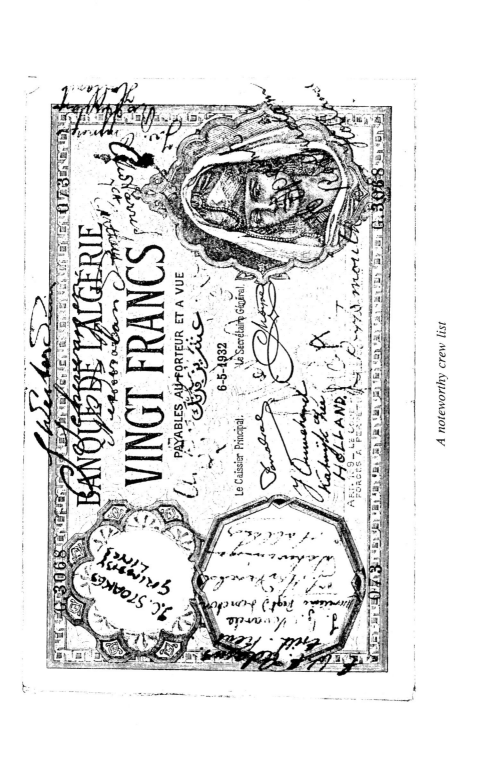

A noteworthy crew list

cushioned the disappointment with the news that at least four of the attackers had been destroyed.

Jack had become active on the crew's behalf in another direction. Inspired by prominent notices displayed around the port, advising servicemen to check their inoculations, he decided it was time we should do so as well.

Enquiries around the ship showed that very few members of the crew had been inoculated against any of the endemic diseases we felt we should seek protection from. An added anxiety was the fear from the condition of one of the firemen that we might already have cholera aboard. With the Captain's approval I went with Sparks to seek what help we could get from the naval and army medical posts who it seemed controlled all the vaccine.

The Royal Navy had none to spare and sent us along to their opposite numbers in khaki, where the sight of strong men occasionally passing out following their needle jabs gave us both pause for thought. In the event the army expressed its regrets and told us they were running short.

Jack and I had much the same experience when we went, with the Captain this time, to see if we could buy some shirts and shorts for the crew. The heat of the summer was building up and with further operations being planned it had seemed like a good idea to equip ourselves with more suitable clothing, a necessity brought home to us during our few days in Tunisia.

Captain Ruig had a commanding presence and we stood back as he put the request to a naval supply branch officer of fairly senior rank only to realise that his gruff shipboard approach was not going down well. Apparently the Royal Navy was having its own problems in getting sufficient equipment and our approach might well have been the last straw.

Nevertheless the officer in charge, so obviously bowed down with his pusser's responsibilities and paperwork, showed a glimmer of sympathy and directed us to his military equivalent. Our Captain by that time had got the bit between his teeth and insisted on leading our small deputation to confront the army.

As Jack and I had previously discovered, such supplications, even when armed with the writ of higher authority, required a gentler touch than we knew to be in our Captain's nature. By now he was out to prove something and we feared the worst. The polite and not unfriendly warrant officer in charge, who was quick to point out that he was also short of supplies, reacted to the Captain's bluff brand of diplomacy very badly. He also turned us down.

Satisfied that he had by now demonstrated that nobody in a position to help was prepared to do so Captain Ruig returned aboard. Treacherously, Jack and I disengaged ourselves, and sneaking back to the army clothing store found the warrant officer expecting us. "I thought you might be back", he said and took our modest list to satisfy as best he could its more urgent requirements.

It was only when we were leaving that he mentioned the Captain. "I'll bet he's a terror at sea," was all he said, but loyally we explained how quickly he grew on one. It was only ashore that he was sometimes misunderstood.

The fact was that Captain Ruig was not the easiest of men to understand, even among that breed of shipmasters conditioned to maintain a traditionally remote role. What may have once been adopted as a protective mask to uphold such solitary responsibility had long since become, I guessed, consolidated in his personality.

There were few members of the crew,. including the deck officers, who had really penetrated beyond that screen, though the Bo'sun, I felt sure, was an exception. Only rarely in all those months, though we had often been alone in the night watches, had I got any glimpse of the man behind that aloof bearing. It might have been a generation gap, but I doubted it.

Other masters in my experience, if only to pass the time or possibly to establish some rapport with their crew, frequently dropped their guard in less formal conversation. Not so with Captain Ruig, although there had been one occasion when for a few minutes only he had revealed his human side. It was in the wheelhouse, during a lull with the enemy in the offing.

By way of encouragement, I thought, he confided it was not only young men who looked bleakly on the prospect of being suddenly blown up or drowned. He had every ambition to survive with just as many things to live for he told me. For more than one reason I was glad to believe him, but the taciturnity as quickly returned. As a complex character Joseph Conrad could have made much of him.

The depth of his feelings for the *ODYSSEUS* if rarely demonstrated could not be doubted, for in spite of her age, undistinguished looks and diminutive size, he was proud of his command, and of the role she was playing. Her cause was his cause and, though the interests of her crew were so closely involved in her fortunes, I do not believe many of them had any doubts as to which came first in his consideration.

Such a crisis was building up in her cramped quarters when the wireless officer and I got back aboard. Whatever infection was going the rounds the ministrations of the mate and the chief steward seemed to be having no effect. Eric's condition had worsened and that of John Westerduin, in the firemen's fo'c'sle, seemed severe. The third mate was also causing concern and other members of the crew had succumbed.

No doctor had been summoned and clearly the Captain believed we could still take care of it ourselves. That night the fireman was so ill we, at one stage, believed he was going to die. It was the gunners, some of whom had also been stricken, who summoned outside help, going aboard the destroyer *LOYAL*, I think, and returning with a naval surgeon.

He eventually set our minds at rest regarding contagious disease and put it down to food poisoning, probably from some of the canned food we had brought out from home. He left strict instructions for the continued treatment of those affected, but ordered the third mate and Joe, the laundryman and former assistant steward, to be removed to hospital.

Captain Ruig accompanied the doctor on his rounds and promised orange juice and lime juice and other items of recommended diet would be supplied to the sick men. It was only the second time I had seen him in the fo'c'sle since leaving Britain and we detected his concern. Jim suspected though that he was just reassuring himself that sufficient members of the crew would be fit to take the ship to sea on schedule for our human cargo was about to be delivered.

There were signs of some improvement the next day, followed by a relapse in some quarters when the mate appeared with a bottle of castor-oil which he sought to administer, but whether on the doctor's advice or on his own initiative was not clear. There was a feeling that he was slightly piqued at outside advice having been sought.

Several ships were loading prisoners-of-war and at one stage the port area had all the appearance of a vast prison camp as Germans and Italians were marched in and slowly, as on a conveyor belt, fed aboard to be distributed in the cargo holds. Our own consignment was brought alongside under an impressive escort of guardsmen, the Coldstreams I think. Even in battledress they managed to put on a ceremonial performance. After handing over their charges to a formidable squad of military police they gave a display which would have done credit to any martial tattoo before parading off.

We were mainly interested in the military force which would sail with us and we were in for a shock. The guardsmen were quickly followed on the scene by a squad of ferocious looking French Moroccan soldiers under an officer especially formidable.

We had done the best we could to ventilate the holds, but the taint of our many acrid cargoes still lingered heavily in that hot atmosphere. The tweendecks, where it had been decided to accommodate them, had been hosed and scrubbed down with deck brooms, but though now reasonably clean offered few concessions to comfort. A working party of German other ranks deposited below many empty oil drums as sanitary provision and containers of freshly baked loaves and cartons of canned food, rations for two days, were later handed down, but that was it.

Our consignment consisting of 450 German officers and thirty Italians, mostly medical officers I think, carried their own blankets. Most had small bundles of personal possessions, but some had none. All had the dishevelled look of defeated men who now wanted to go quietly and, perhaps, as quickly as possible to whatever destination they were bound.

The Italians, particularly one of senior rank who had much to say for himself, were the only ones to put up any show of protest at such mode of transportation, but stern warnings from the Red Caps quickly stifled the brief demonstration. No doubt the sight of the Moroccans, who had by then changed into loose fitting fatigues and were fixing their fiendishly long bayonets, also had something to do with it.

The senior German officer, whose uniform case was carried aboard for him was, I think, allocated some corner of the cabin space amidships. The officer in charge of the escort whose superior role was reflected in the dazzling mirror polish of his knee length boots and Sam Browne, was given the third mate's cabin.

Such niceties were quickly arranged, but for those of us whose task was to close the hatches and batten them down a much more complex consideration had arisen. The stringent regulations which governed the safety of ships at sea, quite rightly insisted that such cargo spaces should be sealed in as watertight a fashion as seamen can contrive.

The thought of so many men consigned for two days to such a dark and ill ventilated prison with no hope of escape in the event of sudden disaster was a thought which disturbed us all, but particularly the mate and the Bo'sun who had to find a speedy compromise. Indeed we all put our heads together to solve the puzzle in such a way as to satisfy the humanitarian compulsion and yet comply as closely as we could with the rigid rules.

After considerable experimentation the Bo'sun at last devised a method, by leaving out sufficient of the thwartships hatchboards and arranging the three layers of heavy tarpaulin over our three broad hatches in such a way as to let in daylight and minimise the risks. Such a louvred effect might have raised official eyebrows, but it satisfied Captain Ruig and certainly relieved our consciences.

Before we sailed, in company with several other ships, there was much martial shouting aboard as the French officer and his N.C.O. marched about the decks posting his sentries who, as far as we could tell, spoke no language but their own strange tongue and seemed to think the members of the crew were also part of their strict surveillance.

The ship's fresh water pump, from which all supplies for washing or drinking had to be drawn, was on the poop where one of our intimidating allies had been posted. Whatever orders he had been given he clearly saw its protection as an important part of his guardianship. When, soon afterwards, one of the crew went along to fill a bucket he was waved away.

Mistaking the gesture for some form of greeting he grinned back and continued to move forward. Instantly the warlike sentinel fixed his long and tapering, four-edged bayonet and presented it with threatening intent. Our shipmate beat a hasty retreat but, even when the French officer had delivered a blistering tirade to the sentry, for the remainder of the trip we approached our fresh water supply with extreme caution.

The sea was not at its best and very soon the pitching decks took their toll. As frightening as they must have been to any enemy on land, the ferocity of the sentries quickly evaporated under an onslaught they had obviously never previously encountered. Though still at their posts most quickly surrendered to the strange experience, lying huddled pathetically in abject misery.

The two exceptions, who took turns through the night on the fo'c'slehead, passed the dark hours making weird and monotonous music on strange bamboo pipes, loudly enough to defeat most attempts at sleep. Yet it seemed a small price to pay in comparison to the inevitable suffering that seasickness must have added to the general misery of our passengers below.

By agreement between the Captain and the officer in charge of the guards the prisoners were allowed to come on deck in small groups during the day. It was left to the senior German officer to organise the rota and the promptness with which he responded indicated that he had some such hope in mind. It seemed he had already worked it out and soon, for twenty minute periods, the captives were taking their turns stretching their legs on our fore and after decks and gulping in the sea air.

At first we kept our distance, but inevitably, as many of them spoke English and in some cases Dutch, curiosity on both sides drew us into conversation. They were mostly young and from their uniforms represented various units of the fierce final stand in Tunisia. There were paratroopers and officers from the Africa Corps in sand-coloured, lightweight drill with leather and canvas boots, and others in grey, tight tunics and riding breeches with boots which were scuffed and losing their shine.

One claimed to have lived in London, another in Manchester. Some claimed to have been stationed in occupied Holland and it was a temptation to some of the Dutch crew, denied news from home for so long, to question them closely. It was Jim, coming off watch, who broke up that conversation by referring grimly to the bombing of his home port as he passed along the deck. It was still his bitterest memory of the war.

One of the prisoners expressed surprise to find us heading west. He told me he expected the *ODYSSEUS* to be heading for Alexandria and the fact that we were sailing in the opposite direction puzzled him. He looked bemused as if realising for the first time that the whole of French North Africa was now Allied territory. It seemed more likely that he was on a fishing expedition, hoping for any useful crumb of information.

That night, with all the prisoners battened down below, the two merciless musicians gave their repertoire a thorough caning, playing a duet which seemed to go on for hours. The sea was much calmer and the rapidly recovering African guards, who had taken up their off-duty abode on the hatch tops, extended the barbaric torture by calling out for more.

The convoy which was making slower progress than anticipated added to the duration of the journey by putting into Algiers Bay the next day. It was busy with shipping, an Atlantic convoy evidently having recently arrived. Many of them were Liberty ships, identical in their light grey paint. For those prisoners having their spell on deck it must have been an eye-opener.

When I told one of them that such ocean vessels were being assembled and launched in a week back in the States, his eyes goggled before he waved a hand in disbelief. Although I could hardly believe it myself, I could see his despondency mounting. He just stood there gazing at them and had to be reminded twice to go below.

After another anxious night at sea and a long, hot day in which the June sun made some of our prisoners glad enough to return to the fetid shade of their world below, we were impatient to reach Oran. Those prisoners who were taking their turn on deck as we approached that port in the late afternoon viewed with ill disguised amazement the largest assembly of American ships we had yet seen in that anchorage.

By the time we went in all the prisoners had been returned to the hold, or so we thought. It was when Jim and I went aft to unlash our coiled mooring ropes which lay on the grating over the steering quadrant, that we found one of them hiding underneath. For his own safety we pulled him out quickly, for if that heavy weight of cast metal had swung over he could have been crushed. Had not the ship been under way it would have been a perfect place of concealment.

There was an expression of relief on his face as he realised the danger he had been in, but there was disappointment in the droop of his shoulders as he was marched away to rejoin the others. An immediate search of the ship uncovered another hopeful escapee playing hide-and-seek elsewhere. It had been their last chance for on the quay, as we went alongside, was a reception committee of American guards, armed to the teeth and looking anxious to get their part of the show on the road.

All the Germans had not stood up to the voyage quite so well. One in particular looked cold and tired and ill. He was one of the older prisoners and told me he had not had a hot drink in many days.

He was not begging. He was just sniffing the faint aroma from the coffee pot in the galley, as if the scent alone might prove sufficiently restorative. On a sudden compassionate impulse, for he was old enough to be my father, I edged him into the empty galley, filled his small pannikin and watched the warmth come back into his face.

From one of his tunic pockets he produced a crumpled, half-empty pack of cigarettes which he thrust towards me. It was all he had to give, he said. When I shook my head and told him it was on the house he apologised for any embarrassment he had caused, smiled his thanks and slipped quietly away. I was not surprised a little later on to find other members of the crew making coffee for some of the more groggy of our departing passengers.

It was a longer process getting them ashore than embarking them. Perhaps it had something to do with the paper work which the Americans so often seemed to require. But gradually the long queue of army trucks and trailers were filled up and sometime after midnight the last of our prisoners-of-war had been driven off into the night. A working party had been sent aboard to unload the oil drums which had fulfilled so necessary a function during the voyage, but we knew when the daylight came there would be another big cleaning operation in the holds.

Our French colonial guards had melted away without ceremony or farewell soon after the Americans had taken over. When we discovered that one of our four motherless kittens, those abandoned by the cat we had acquired from the American ship, had disappeared we guessed it had been taken by one of them rather than by any of the prisoners. In contrast to their fierce demeanour the guards had shown a keen and gentle interest in the furry orphans. They were fascinated by them.

The cook, who had also shown us a hidden side to his normally unsmiling nature when he had adopted them, was particularly upset. The kittens, three black and one grey, had thrived on his fostering, though more cynical members of the crew thought his great pride in them might have had something to do with their ready appreciation of his cooking.

It was good to have the ship to ourselves again and the clearing up after the prisoners departure was undertaken with some zeal. It was hastily done because the Americans were anxious to start work in the lower holds, loading cargo now piled high on the quays. It was a clear indication that the build-up of arms and equipment in strategic ports to the east, for the Allies' next offensive thrust, was well under way.

We found the holds littered with discarded sketch maps of Algeria and Morocco as testimony to the vain hopes of last minute escape. I was not surprised when Jim told me that one of the Germans waiting to go ashore had produced a wad of French banknotes and tried to bribe him into finding him some place of concealment. He had mistaken Jim for a Frenchman and seemed hurt at his reply.

It was hot and dusty in Oran and the sickness which had hit the crew since we left Bizerta was still prevalent. Two of the gunners, lying in cramped quarters where even the slightest illness would have been hard to bear, looked bad indeed. After a quick examination a naval doctor immediately ordered their removal ashore. Within two days two of the others who had been struck down were also taken out of the ship.

The cook who, apart from the occasion in Algiers when he had gone ashore to escape the Bo'sun's wrath, had not had a day off duty since leaving Britain now started to complain of feeling unwell. The loading of the ship was proceeding apace and it would only be a matter of two or three days before the *ODYSSEUS* would be sailing again. Captain Ruig seemed strangely unconcerned.

My own medical problems which had for so long been in abeyance, mainly through circumstance over which I had little control and an extended optimism on my part, had become of increasing concern. The Captain had promised to arrange for an expert consultation ashore. When I asked him about it he told me it had slipped his mind and asked me to make my own arrangements, suggesting that I first went to the Ministry of War Transport Office to enlist their help.

It seemed all too casual a way to seek expert reassurance, but time was running out. The next day when I discovered that an appointment had been arranged with someone at the American army medical centre in the port, I was in two minds about keeping it. It was perhaps the recollection that the doctor I had seen there previously had been an impressive product of that hospital of international renown, the John Hopkins in Baltimore, which decided my fate.

The same man was waiting to see me and in that admirable and meticulous American style was still able to produce his original notes. He examined me thoroughly, questioned me explicitly and at length, and seemed surprised that I had not been back before. He made a lot more notes before writing down the recommendation which would part me from the *ODYSSEUS* irrevocably within two more days. It was his decree that I should be returned to Britain as quickly as possible for expert attention and proper treatment.

The thought of the Captain's reaction occupied my mind as I walked back to the ship in some state of shock, but my deepest concern was over those close companions I was going to miss and the ship whose discomforts and adventures compounded the odyssey which I could not deny still held me in thrall. The more serious implications occurred to me later.

CHAPTER SIXTEEN

Captain Ruig, never demonstratively sympathetic, took the news without pleasure, but whether that was because of my medical condition or due to the fact that he would now have to find a replacement, was not clear. I guessed it was the latter and volunteered to delay my departure until a substitute was found.

It was not until the following day therefore that I presented my medical report and recommendations to those officials ashore who had requested them. What followed might have been amusing, but for the circumstances. Clearly taken aback by my news the two officials involved, one representing the Department of War Transport and the other a Sea Transport officer in commander's uniform, held a hasty conference on which the outcome of the war might well have depended.

It was the one in uniform, an obvious product of the school that believed that anyone who could still walk was not to be spared, who ruled that I should be thoroughly examined again. If I had gone there for entertainment it was one of the better moments, an unexpected spectacle of wartime bureaucracy plunging into the minefield of medical etiquette.

This time they arranged an appointment for me to be seen by a doctor at the Royal Naval medical post. I was only too happy to co-operate, for a second opinion was more than I had requested and was not to be sneezed at. If I was annoyed at all it was because, up to that stage, little concern had been expressed for the patient. The naval trawler base was a considerable distance away and it took me some time to arrange a lift in a jeep.

As I had anticipated, the naval surgeon blew up when he realised what was being asked of him. But he examined me again at my request, questioned me at length and made out his own certificate. It was brief and to the point: "This man is unfit for sea service and should be sent back to the U.K. to be medically overhauled." Only then did he ask me for the American doctor's certificate and promised to return it to me that afternoon.

He looked grim and told me he was going over to the Sea Transport office to present his report in person and I would have given much to have been present. Later in the day I got the gist, as much as medical etiquette would allow, of what had transpired and noted another victory to be chalked up in North Africa. But if red tape had been the loser I was not too happy about how it left me.

When I got back to the ship I turned to for there was much to do and a crisis of another sort brewing. The hatches had been closed and the American army dockers were in the process of adding a deck cargo to her load.

It was no ordinary deck cargo and consisted of a great many heavy steel, cubiform tanks stacked on top of each other, almost completely blocking both fore and after decks. They were the component parts of a Rhino barge and, locked together, would eventually form a pontoon obviously intended for invasion purposes in the forthcoming operation which no-one now doubted was targeted on Sicily.

The urgency to move such heavy equipment along the coast to those ports from which the thrust would eventually begin had obviously had some bearing on the over optimistic assessment of the ship's capacity by an inexperienced loading officer. In normal times the cargo plan of a ship falls to the responsibility of the mate, but in war operations it was strictly in the hands of the military planners.

The deck cargo was a serious mistake. Not only did it make the fo'c'sle accommodation almost inaccessible and a positive death trap, it made free passage on the decks so difficult as to be highly dangerous to life and limb and the safe management of the ship. But there was a much more serious consideration. Her centre of gravity was now so high in relation to her buoyancy factor it required little understanding of the most elementary rules of ship stability to realise her equilibrium was in danger.

The Captain had been ashore and later in the day a Dutch seaman, who was quick to reveal his home port as Rotterdam, came aboard as my replacement. For me there were some documents to check with the second mate and forms to sign. It was the moment to say my farewells which I didn't relish.

I felt suddenly that growing emotional pang of leaving home. He was smiling as he handed over my discharge and, barely disguising his envy, wished me well. The mate, twinkling his approval, gave me a warm handshake and hoped we would meet again, soon. Members of the engineroom staff called out their good wishes and the gunners added a cheer. I was inundated with hastily scribbled addresses and promised to contact families and friends in Britain.

The Bo'sun smiling broadly almost crushed my hand in his bear-like paw and the cook smiled as if to say all had been forgiven. Albert, his assistant, still waiting for his first letter from home, asked me not to forget to try and do something about the mail. Both Jacobs, who saw in my unexpected departure a new hope of release for others, told me where I might find them one day in London.

I already knew, for Jim van Ommeren had already got my assurance that I would accompany him before long down the Marylebone Road to take in Madame Tussaud's and go on to Speaker's Corner.

My parting with Captain Ruig was as formal as had been our first meeting, but then he had much on his mind. He was anxious to check that I had signed a proper receipt for the documents that severed my connection with the company, but did not mention the news which Jack had earlier confided. That morning a signal had been received confirming that reliefs for some other members of the crew were on their way out from Britain.

By that time experience had taught the crew of the *ODYSSEUS* that such tidings only became credible when they actually happened and I could understand why, apart from telling me, Jack had kept such momentous news to himself. It could have explained the Captain's silence on the exciting expectation. I hoped also, even if it came to pass, that those who were not to be replaced would not be too crestfallen.

Joe Stoakes, who had so readily humped my gear when I first came aboard, shouldered it again as cheerfully as ever and, with Eric and Jack Ridler, followed me down the gangway where a truck was waiting to take me and my luggage to some sort of hotel. As I climbed in beside the driver I heard some more baggage being thrown in the back and was immediately joined by the Dutchman intended as my replacement.

He had decided not to accept the offer. Looking back at the ship I saw Jim van Ommeren smiling broadly under his cap and guessed he had not been able to resist the compulsion to mark a fellow Rotterdam seaman's card. Sadly, the sight of the ill-loaded *ODYSSEUS* with her top heavy deck cargo seemed reason enough to make any sailor want to beat an immediate retreat.

He had not wasted his opportunity though for the steward, a man of generous impulse when stores were available, on hearing of the hungry conditions ashore had provided fresh bread and a collection of canned food to sustain us for a while. I was to be glad of it.

I didn't expect to see the *ODYSSEUS* again. She had been due to sail during the night and I had little doubt that her deck cargo, or some substantial part of it would have been removed by that time. But the next day, seeing her masts and funnel top just visible above the long sheds masking her berth, I returned to the scene.

To my great astonishment I found her still loaded high, incongruously like something future generation of seafarers of more prosaic mind might have mistaken for a container ship. Having seen how she had been loaded below her hatches, with so disproportionate a weight in her tweendecks as to have already made her exceedingly tender, the plight of her crew brought immediate dismay.

It turned to alarm when I saw armed sentries at the gangway and realised they were there to prevent anyone boarding or leaving the ship. I was made to stand well back, but sailors have lusty voices and I was quickly informed of dramatic events during the night. For some unexplained reason, perhaps to make a point, Captain Ruig had given instructions for the ship to sail at 3.00am and could not have been more surprised when his crew walked ashore.

What the Sea Transport office made of it could only be imagined, but "mutiny" must have been an early reaction even though every one of the ship's officers had been equally involved. It explained the presence of the sentries but there was nothing, unless it was chairborne pride, to explain why the dangerous state of the ship's stability had neither been acknowledged nor corrected.

It had been a harrowing time in other ways for the crew. Because of the exceptionally swift loading of the ship the coal to top up her bunkers had arrived late and much of it was still piled on deck, waiting to be shovelled down below, when the Arab trimmers were sent ashore. A fresh meat supply, not often or easily come by, had arrived about the same time, but because the ice with which to preserve it had not been delivered it was rapidly going off in the hot conditions.

The galley was out of action, closed up because of the bunkering, and no-one got an evening meal. More seriously, a section of the steering gear along the deck remained impeded by the coal. They were all matters which the crew could, and doubtless would have taken in their stride if only the wholly inexplicable order to sail had been appropriately rescinded.

All of these things and others relating to the events of the night were to be written down by Jack Ridler at the request of the Bo'sun and other members of the crew, and the two page document, neatly typed, duly submitted to the local Ministry of War Transport representative. Copies of the deposition which had been signed by those involved, were addressed also to the M.O.W.T. chief in Algiers and to the Nederlands Shipping and Trading Commission in London.

In the meantime the ridiculous impasse remained, with the obvious and increasingly urgent solution staring officialdom in the face.

In the event it was the ship's crew which resolved the issue. I regretted I was not there to witness it but the American army, though not unsympathetic, had been dutifully firm in observing the orders to move me along. It was one of the gunners, also waiting for a ship home, who witnessed the dramatic denouement and was there to tell me about it when I went to the quay the next morning and saw the *ODYSSEUS* had gone.

My immediate and alarming suspicion was that she had attempted to sail and had probably capsized in the bay. The real facts were just as Homeric. The crew, weary of the intransigence ashore, and to prove their contention that the ship was so unstable as to be unsafe, had later the previous day decided to demonstrate it.

They put on their lifejackets, made ready for sea and were only waiting for the pilot, who must have been a brave man indeed, when the ship took a sudden heavy list to port to hover there perilously. To the relief of her Captain and crew, particularly the engineroom staff, her centre of gravity must have still been low enough to start the swing back, but the fact that her moorings were still in place had much to do with it.

It was a hair-raising moment and the danger was not over. As she rolled back through the point of balance and towards the quay those on the dockside, including a Sea Transport office, fled in all directions. As if making her own protest at such ill-usage, *ODYSSEUS* came to rest with her boatdeck jammed against the wall and lay there precariously posed.

The strained wires and taut hemp which held the ship at such an undignified angle were quickly doubled up to prolong the embrace. Then, with all the alacrity previously withheld, the top layer of excessive weight was at last removed. With something remarkably like a sigh the *ODYSSEUS* gradually recovered her equilibrium.

If triumph had been uppermost in anyone's mind that would have been the proper moment for one of her crew to have hoisted the three alphabetical code flags "Q-E-D". I guessed that in the general state of shock following their narrow escape, not even Jack had thought of that.

The main thing was that the *ODYSSEUS* was back in circulation and with the preparations for Operation "Husky", the invasion of Sicily, her participation in it was assured. When she left Oran she was bound for Sousse one of the smaller ports beyond Tunis from which part of the vast armada would eventually sail.

Though the control of the operation had meant the transfer of naval and military headquarters to Malta, Algiers and Oran were to continue in importance for the re-routing of ships and the transhipment of cargoes. Before the build-up was complete the *ODYSSEUS* pursued her coastal voyages unremittingly with only one incident to change the individual hopes and expectations of her crew.

The crew replacements, so long anticipated or rumoured, actually arrived, but in such reduced number as to bring disappointment to a considerable proportion of her over burdened, long-suffering, yet persevering crew. The deck officers and engineers, and the steward were able to hand over to their substitutes, but the Bo'sun, sailors, firemen and other engineroom crew were less well provided for.

Jacob Ouwehand and Eric Adams and the Bo'sun were among those who learned they would have to stay on. Albert Bolton who had joined as galley boy was another, and for some unexplained reason the wireless officer had also been overlooked. Jack Ridler, who by that time could certainly be forgiven for losing some of his enchantment with his first engagement, would have to continue his isolated existence in the lonely caboose on the boatdeck.

Captain Ruig, whose preference for the Mediterranean climate had long been accepted, had no doubt been wise not to broadcast the fact that the transfusion had never been intended to be complete. He and Sparks would be the only two veterans of the outward voyage to sit at the saloon table, but I had little hope that it would instill any greater warmth to their formal relationship.

It was an irony of the situation - for I felt that if I had not already left the ship I too might have stayed on - that I did not get a passage to Britain for almost two months, arriving back in the same convoy as those who were later relieved.

It was an arduous period in which I got no medical attention at all and was to wish more than once that I could have found myself being awakened in the *ODYSSEUS*'s cramped fo'c'sle. Shipped eventually from Oran to Gibraltar in the bare tweendecks of a Liberty ship, in the company of other seafarers and a battalion of British infantry, I experienced over two nights something of what our Axis prisoners had endured.

From Gibraltar after further delays we embarked in the Cunarder *SAMARIA*. Though I did not know it then, Joe Stoakes, Jim van Ommeren and others from the crew of the *ODYSSEUS* were aboard another crowded trooper waiting to sail in the same fast convoy. I was soon to meet up with some of them again in London and to hear in detail of the events I had missed.

It was not long either before Eric and Jack and even Jacob Ouwehand were in touch, reporting cryptically on the latest adventures of the ship which was much in my mind. The news of the Sicilian invasion had come whilst I was in Gibraltar and I had no doubt that the *ODYSSEUS* would have been involved in the back up. Though the Allies now controlled so much more of the Mediterranean the striking power of the Axis from the air was as formidable as ever.

The Luftwaffe and the Regia Aeronautica kept up their attacks of the past nine months with unflagging urgency and concentrated determination. U-boats, and to some extent E-boats, were still active and mines had become an increased hazard. I wondered how much longer the *ODYSSEUS* with her reduced speed, perfidious cargoes and constant exposure could rely on her luck.

More than 2,500 ships of the Royal Navy, the United States Navy and the Allied merchant fleets took part in the invasion of Sicily, sailing from Malta and both sides of the Mediterranean. Over 180,000 British, Commonwealth and American troops were landed there with the need to be immediately sustained by the cargo carriers, often anchored within less than forty miles of the nearest enemy airfields.

In such a vast company the odds in favour of the small *ODYSSEUS* undoubtedly increased. When the ports of Syracuse and Augusta were taken by the British Eighth Army after heavy fighting she was soon able to go alongside and, for Jack Ridler, there came a bonus to cancel any disappointment he might have felt at not being replaced. The months of being denied news from home were forgotten too in a surprising family reunion.

Having last heard of his two brothers from Egypt or the Western Desert, where they were serving in the first formation of the S.A.S., he pricked up his ears on hearing that men of that cloak-and-dagger service had been spiking enemy guns in the locality the day before. His search in the neighbourhood where there had been some sharp action was joyously rewarded when he found his brothers Duncan and Freddy, duty done, relaxing in an olive grove. Their astonishment must have been immense.

The successful landings were not without casualties offshore. In the run up to the invasion U-boats had been particularly active. The *CITY OF VENICE*, the Ellerman Line ship, whose anti-aircraft fire we had been so grateful for in Philippeville many months before, was hit in one of her forward holds by a German torpedo. Her bridge was shattered and one of her lifeboats destroyed and she began to settle.

Pre-War picture of Ellerman's CITY OF VENICE (8,800 grt) which survived earlier bombing attacks only to be sunk by U-boat torpedo in the central Mediterranean whilst bound for Sicily - one of nearly 40 ships of the company's fleet lost in the War.
(Courtesy of W.S.S.)

Her combustible cargo quickly burst into flames and soon she was blazing from stem to stern. Apart from the war cargo she had loaded in the Clyde she had 302 servicemen aboard and a crew of 180. All managed to get away safely, but twenty men were lost including her Captain when their boat was overturned by one of the rescue ships.

Another ship on the same mission, the South American Saint Line's *ST ESSYLT* was torpedoed and lost at the same time. The following day the commodore ship of the convoy, the *DEVIS* owned by Lamport & Holt was sunk, probably by the same U-boat. Such severe loss was a grim signal of the enemy's determination to keep the fight at its full intensity.

But it was the counter attacks from the air on the Sicilian ports and anchorages which were most savage. Syracuse and Augusta took a great deal of the punishment as the enemy recovered from the early shock. Ropner's *FORT PELLY*, unloading ammunition, was hit by a stick of bombs when both German and Italian bombers attacked from the sea.

She disintegrated with a violence that killed thirty-eight of her crew and injured many more. The *EMPIRE FLORIZEL*, one of J. & C. Harrison's ships, blew up in a sheet of flame after receiving two direct hits, her cargo of case petrol burning for many hours. Another ship, the *OCEAN VIRTUE* was severely damaged by a near miss and the port of Augusta was left in a shambles.

One ship which escaped, the *EMPIRE MOON*, sailed with her coal cargo in search of a safer anchorage, but was torpedoed the same night by a U-boat lying in wait off the southerly tip of the island. She was later towed into Syracuse where her cargo was salvaged after she sank.

That port came in for some particularly fierce raids in the Germans' counter attack. Ropner's *FISHPOOL*, carrying thousands of tons of ammunition and aviation fuel in drums, was set ablaze and exploded killing twenty-eight of her crew including her Captain and several servicemen, with many wounded. As in North Africa the men of the Royal Engineers dock companies were quickly in the thick of it.

Some of them, whose expertise was a vital factor in the success of the operation were recent survivors from a disaster which might easily have imperilled part of it. They had embarked at Sfax in Tunisia shortly before the invasion in the converted liner *YOMA* which was serving as a transport. She was torpedoed by a U-boat north-east of Benghazi and sank by the stern within minutes. She was crowded with troops of whom nearly 500, many of them pre-war professional dockers, were drowned. Her Captain and thirty-two of her crew also died.

In the heat of such determined resistance even the brightly lit and boldly identified hospital ships were not immune. The converted British India liner *TALAMBA*, serving in that capacity, was bombed and sunk off Syracuse whilst loading wounded. When Sicily had been cleared and the Allied armies moved on to the Italian mainland in early September, first at Reggio and Taranto and soon afterwards at Salerno, the ferocity from the air continued.

It was at Salerno that another hospital ship, Furness Withy's *NEWFOUNDLAND*, was hit twice by aerial torpedoes. She had no wounded aboard, but many of her crew and medical staff were among the twenty-three who died. It was there, too, that the enemy introduced an ingenious and fiendish radio controlled glider bomb, adding a startling new menace to merchant ships and warships alike.

During the invasion of Sicily, Radio Officer Jack Ridler had a surprise reunion with his two younger brothers, members of the same S.A.S. unit relaxing after an overnight operation. Jack is in the centre with Duncan to his right and Freddy on the left.

The dramatic surrender of the Italian fleet at Malta and the news, following Mussolini's downfall, that Italy was on the brink of changing its allegiance to the Allied cause brought temporary elation to the crew of the *ODYSSEUS*. But they soon found that its main effect was to intensify the Germans' determination to impede or destroy the maritime supply lines on which the Allied armies supremely relied. For her the war was far from over.

CHAPTER SEVENTEEN

The advance on Naples, following the landings at Salerno, took longer than anticipated. Without a major deep water port in which trans-Atlantic cargoes and those from Britain could be directly discharged, the transhipment of the campaign's supplies through the main ports of North Africa was to continue for some time.

For the heterogeneous fleet of small merchantmen now diverted to extended routes, the toil and hazards persisted. Their shallower draughts and proven versatility made them indispensable serving the smaller ports which had rapidly fallen under Allied control in southeast Italy.

It was also a factor in their retention that the fleets of landing craft, used with such success in the assault on Sicily and at Salerno, were mainly required at home in preparation for the inevitable invasion of Europe across the English Channel. Though some were retained for the assault at Anzio to the south of Rome, the urgent need for their return ahead of D-day was a priority which left the long serving Allied steamers and motor coasters to fulfil their still perilous role.

Some were to remain in the Mediterranean theatre almost until the end of the war. Others like the ferry *EMPIRE DACE* of barely 700 gross tons, which had caused the crew of the *ODYSSEUS* much concern on the voyage out, would not return at all.

Sadly that remarkable vessel, which had so gallantly and successfully helped blaze the trail for the later fleet of purpose-built tank landing ships, was sunk by a mine with heavy loss of life at Missilonghi in the Gulf of Patras, after the Allied landings in Greece the following year.

At that period in her career the closest the *ODYSSEUS* was to come to those shores, or to her legendary namesake's home island of Ithaka, was in late November 1943 when she skirted the Ionian Sea to steam into the Adriatic. She was bound for Barletta, a port not far to the south of the mountainous battle line where the German and Allied armies were locked in combat.

If the crew had anything to celebrate it was the grimy nature of their cargo. For the first time since she had been loaded in Britain for her outward voyage to the Mediterranean the *ODYSSEUS* carried nothing in her holds more dangerously inflammable or highly explosive than coal. To those who, for more than a year, had been constantly

Adriatic

TERMOLI

CASSINO

C.GARGANO

FOGGIA

BARLETTA

BARI

BRINDISI

NAPLES

SALERNO

TARANTO

Tyrrhenian Sea

Ionian Sea

PALERMO

MESSINA

REGGIO

C. SPARTIVENTO

Sicily

AUGUSTA

SYRACUSE

SCALE   1inch = 60 miles

Mediterranean

Malta (G.C)

14° E

16° E

18°

conscious of that volcanic threat, the thunder of the gritty cargo pouring into her holds had been sweet music indeed.

It was of prime importance nonetheless, urgently needed to keep power stations running and to bunker the coal burning minesweepers, those former trawlers whose never ceasing and perilous duties provided much needed protection from a deadly and indiscriminate threat.

DEVON COAST (646 grt) sank at Bari, Italy after catching fire following the air attack on December 2, 1943. She and the DORSET COAST, sunk at Algiers in May that year, were the smallest of the British cargo ships serving in the Mediterranean.
(Courtesy of W.S.S.)

For those who were anticipating their second Christmas in that theatre of war such a bonus had come as a welcome and not inappropriate seasonal present. But the euphoria was not to last long. There was a price to pay. At Barletta the crew discovered that the *ODYSSEUS* was to be deployed for use as a lure in a Commando operation against an enemy outpost on the coastal flank beyond Cape Gargano.

It was to be a combined "fishing" expedition involving not only soldiers but air force personnel equipped to direct Allied planes on to the target once it had been pinpointed. They were to be embarked in motorised wooden schooners to merge with the traditional local scenery. The *ODYSSEUS* and her crew were to be the bait on which the hopes of an enemy reaction would depend.

Whether it was a concealed gun battery or just a key enemy observation post the Commando force intended to deal with was not revealed. When the *ODYSSEUS* steamed north from Barletta, followed at an appropriate distance by her picturesque satellites, there was an atmosphere of suppressed excitement aboard. Though the feeling of exposure was no novel experience, the sense of vulnerability grew stronger once she had rounded the mountainous cape and altered course to the west to hug the coast.

The hours passed and nothing happened and by the time she was approaching the small harbour of Termoli, some eighty miles beyond Barletta, the signal came for her to return. The enemy had either pulled out or was not biting.

If there was disappointment it was among the Commandos and the others in the tailing schooners. There was a distinct sense of relief aboard the steamer and it was a more relaxed crew which put back into Barletta. They were not to stay there long. Captain Ruig was instructed to take her to the larger port of Bari, forty miles down the coast towards the heel of Italy, to wait for further orders.

She arrived there late in the day on 2nd December and was given a berth at a mole in the outer harbour whose congested waters indicated the recent arrival of a large convoy directly from the United States. There were also many ships, newly discharged, awaiting departure, and against the inner quays under the dock cranes and blazing arc-lights other ocean vessels were being unloaded.

Such blatant illumination was unusual, demonstrating not only the urgency of the operation to land and distribute so much war material, but also the supreme confidence in the port's air defences. Such intense activity, with so little attempt to conceal it so long after sundown, might easily have suggested to those who did not know better that the Luftwaffe no longer posed a threat.

There was good enough reason for the hustle and for the queue of heavily laden ships awaiting their turn. Bari had become not only the main strategic supply port for the Allied armies in the east of Italy, but also for the American Fifteenth Airforce, recently transferred from Tunisia to nearby Italian airfields.

Many of those ships were laden with bombs, artillery and tank ammunition, and with them were tankers waiting to unload heavy consignments of aviation fuel. More easily recognisable among the many Liberty ships and the large British transports were the smaller vessels of the long serving campaign fleet to which *ODYSSEUS* belonged, ships also flying the national flags of Norway and Poland and the British red ensign.

Still looking strangely out of place so far from their home shores were the doughty *DEVON COAST* and *BRITTANY COAST* of Liverpool. If there was complacency in Bari that night it was not shared by the crews of such ships to whom alertness had for so long been the first rule of survival. Yet there was an air to that scene unlike that of earlier months at such ports as Algiers, Bougie, Philippeville and Bone where nightly attacks had been anticipated with positive assumption.

Perhaps it was the lights which inspired the atmosphere of unusual confidence, or the knowledge that the area now abounded in airfields which had brought the Allies that supremacy the enemy no longer enjoyed. Whatever it was, and whether it was real or fancied, the fact remained that Bari, the main supply base, was by any strategy of warfare a prime target for determined attack.

The North African campaign had been a war of supply lines which the enemy had lost. In all those raids over all those months it had failed to put any Allied port out of action. In Italy the concentration of ships and supplies at Bari had not escaped its attention. It was now ready to try again.

In the week before, over several days, the contrails of reconnaissance planes had been seen high in the blue skies over Bari. It was not unusual and had apparently aroused no unwonted reaction to impending danger. It would have been the only clue to the machinations of a still powerful enemy keenly fighting for time, yet patient enough to make sure the net was full before making its strike.

On 2nd December, with every berth occupied and hardly an empty mooring, the port of Bari contained the largest assembled collection of the Allies' vital war supplies they were ever likely to find on those shores. If Britain's Fleet Air Arm attack on the Italian fleet at nearby Taranto three years before, or the Japanese attack on the American fleet at Pearl Harbour in December 1941 had impressed the

Luftwaffe, they were operations it now intended to reproduce that night on the congregated Allied merchant fleet at Bari.

From its airfields in Northern Italy the powerful force of Junkers-88's, perhaps 100 or more, swept down the Adriatic in the early evening, the sinister beat of its engines lost over an empty sea. It was nearing 7.30pm as the leaders altered course to approach the brightly lit port from the east flying almost at sea level. If those in charge of Bari's defences had been relying on any early warning system they were confounded that night.

Aboard the *ODYSSEUS* the evening meal was over. Captain Ruig was in the saloon playing cards with some of his officers. The watch on deck heard the sound of an aircraft engine above the noise of the cargoes being discharged in the inner harbour. Instinctively he pressed the alarm bell which might well have been the first warning Bari got that night. Not that it mattered, for moments later a parachute flare burst above bringing its dire message.

It was quickly followed by others as the roar of low flying bombers drowned all other sounds as the leaders began the attack. The brightly lit quays lined with ships made the flares scarcely necessary at that stage and the port lights were still burning as the first bombs burst beyond the inner harbour. By the time the anti-aircraft fire had opened up, spasmodically at first, the next wave was finding its target among the ships and harbour installations and soon there were fires enough to make any lingering cargo lights irrelevant.

The intensity of the attack and its accuracy quickly brought to the nightmarish scene the realisation of the real peril threatening all. As closely packed, burning ships broke from their mooring to endanger their neighbours the fear of interactive disaster was only too evident. As the raiders came in with hardly a pause to unload their incendiary and high explosive bombs most ships found themselves in a trap.

The *ODYSSEUS* was in trouble soon after the raid started. Her gunners fought back with a determination which, in the past, must have deflected more than one enemy pilot from his purpose yet at Bari seemed to have little effect on that constant stream of planes adding their deadly contributions to the encroaching havoc.

Some came in so low it seemed at times they would meet disaster in the blast from their own bomb loads. She sustained the first damage to add to her many scars as four bombs exploded in the water not far away. The next stick landed with one bomb bursting close on her port side with shattering effect.

It was as if some giant fist had struck in a last furious attempt to crush her completely. In a deafening instant her guns had become silent and her survival seemed to hang in the balance. The devastation to her upper decks, swept so savagely months before, was again only a blurred impression in the first moments of shock as she listed heavily to starboard.

It was as she righted herself as if testing her traumatised frame that the extent of the damage and injuries to her crew became quickly apparent. A quick check showed that no-one had been killed, but the saloon soon looked like a casualty station as those with blast and splinter wounds were treated and temporarily patched by the new second mate, E. de Blaauw.

For the mate and the Bo'sun, Jacob Ouwehand, Eric Adams and other members of the crew the urgent task was finding out if her remarkable iron plates had once again sufficiently defied the enormous blast to keep her afloat. Holds had to be inspected and wells sounded and heads were shaken in astonishment and admiration for the *ODYSSEUS* showed no sign of any serious damage below her water line.

Captain Ruig who had suffered a severe blow to the head greeted the news with grim satisfaction. Above that level it was an altogether different picture. In the moments of near disaster her claims to the nickname of *S.S. "Pepperpot"* had increased twofold. Apart from the fret of new gashes along her topsides, above her maindeck she had all the appearance of having been to a breaker's yard.

Most of her deck fittings had been crushed, ripped through by bomb splinters, or torn from their bolts and mountings and blown over the side. Heavy wooden doors had been ripped from their hinges and lay about like shattered matchwood. Cabins and bulkheads had been gashed open as if by some Titan with a colossal can-opener.

Above all, where her funnel should have been was now only shocking space revealing the livid sky. All that remained of that once imposing and most important centrepiece was the crushed and jagged stump outlined against the background of leaping flames.

It was a crippling bow, for the *ODYSSEUS* depended entirely on her tall smoke stack for the natural draught to maintain the furnace heat which was the source of her steam power. She had survived for the moment, but as the last of the bombers roared away from the holocaust state, she would still need the most extraordinary luck to escape the mounting aftermath.

By that time the port of Bari must have been seen from above as a glowing, even brilliant, testimonial to the Luftwaffe's striking power. But for those engulfed in the smoke and flames there was much worse to come. Many ships had been hit and many were burning soon to be drifting out of control, and added to the peril of so much eruptive cargo was an expanding oil slick from a shattered harbour pipeline.

The first ammunition ship to explode in what was to become a chain of destruction was the American Liberty ship *JOHN L. MOTLEY*. Her cataclysmic end with the loss of all aboard instantly settled the fate of a sister ship, the *JOHN BASCOM* already blazing and abandoned and drifting down on her from alongside. Another Liberty ship set ablaze was the *SAMUEL J. TILDEN* carrying a deck cargo of aviation fuel in drums. Lost with her was a consignment of medical supplies and hospital equipment urgently needed ashore, particularly that night and in the days to come.

There soon came an even more violent eruption as another fiercely burning American merchant ship, drifting out of control, disintegrated with appalling effect. She was the *JOHN HARVEY* which had been carrying in one of her holds a secret cargo which was to add immensely to the deadly nature of the contaminated effusion now spreading its way across the harbour. Unknown to all but a few, who were to die before its disclosure, she carried in one of her holds a consignment of mustard gas bombs.

Apparently intended as a precautionary reserve, against the contingency of an enemy ever resorting to such desperate measures, their contents released instantly in the blast quickly poisoned the oily water. In those areas where the toxic solution burned fiercely, its fumes polluted the air. Its contamination, unsuspected at first, added tragically to the already heavy death-role.

The massive explosion which filled the sky with bursting ammunition in a startling variety of colours, caused widespread damage, danger, death and injury, and produced a tidal wave which spread the surface fires of burning oil and in places swept huddled survivors from precarious refuge on the outer moles.

The British ship *TESTBANK*, hemmed in by other burning vessels nearby was an immediate victim, being virtually torn apart by the blast which killed seventy of her crew. The violent interaction was to be repeated throughout the stricken port.

When the Liberty ship *JOSEPH WHEELER*, with 8,000 tons of munitions aboard, blew up with the loss of all hands the British *FORT ATHABASKA* was set ablaze. The intense heat of the flames caused the explosion of two captured German rocket missiles she was to have taken to Britain for expert examination, shattering her hull and killing most of her crew.

LOM - one of the many Norwegian ships engaged in the hazardous shuttle service, was one of 17 Allied cargo carriers lost in the Bari raid.
(Courtesy of W.S.S.)

The small Norwegian steamer *LOM* in whose company the *ODYSSEUS* had frequently sailed, blew up in a flash of brilliant green light immediately sinking the already blazing, small motor tanker *DEVON COAST*. Her crew had abandoned her just in time, but several of them were to suffer the effects of the mustard gas as a result of their immersion.

There were other ships sunk that night, several of them belonging to the closely bonded fleet of smaller supply ships. Among those lost were the Norwegian *BOLLSTA* and *NORLOM*, the *LARS*

KRUSE under the British flag, and the Polish *PUCK* and *LWOW*. The last two, which had suffered in the close attack which had so disabled the *ODYSSEUS*, and were soon to catch fire, lay at anchor with sterns moored to the mole only a short distance away.

Both were loaded with mixed cargoes of cased petrol and ammunition, with which the crew of the *ODYSSEUS* was only too familiar, and represented imminent danger should their fires get out of control. But with a dozen or more seriously injured men aboard there were more immediate concerns for those aboard the Dutch ship.

Fortunately although the starboard lifeboat had been wrecked by the bomb blast, the motor boat in the port davits had escaped serious damage and as a priority it was decided to ferry the wounded across to the mole. There was a stone blockhouse at the seaward end which promised some security from any further explosions.

It was only during that operation that Eric Adams became aware of the added danger from mustard gas. The smell of garlic coming from some of the damp clothing of the men who had already found shelter on the mole alerted him to it very quickly and he was later surprised to learn it had taken so long for some doctors ashore to detect it.

NORLOM - A wartime picture of another of the three Norwegian ships
sunk in the devastating attack on Bari.
(Courtesy of W.S.S.)

Back aboard the *ODYSSEUS* the situation had become more critical. One of the ammunition ships was now burning fiercely and little warning was needed to know it was about to explode. The blast came quickly inflicting more damage to the ship and wounding more members of the crew, but by good fortune or some strange quirk of eruptive inconsistency, the main force of the blow cleared her masts, depositing the red hot debris in waters beyond.

Suddenly a new danger presented itself. The flames on the water, which at times had leapt to a height of fifty feet, began to move quickly in the ship's direction. The cold night air rapidly grew warmer as the blazing oil under a curtain of smoke moved towards the *ODYSSEUS* like a prairie fire.

Jack Ridler, whose introduction to the *ODYSSEUS* had been in the port of Barry in South Wales, had until a few hours before been looking forward to the more alluring prospect of visiting its Adriatic namesake. Viewing the calamitous scene with its ominous portents the irony of the situation did not escape him. But there was little time for such reflection.

The decision was taken to launch one of the ship's undamaged rafts to allow more of the crew with the additional wounded to join the others on the mole. It almost led to a disaster. However hard the able bodied plied their inadequate paddles a strong and perverse current pulled them relentlessly towards the flames.

Eventually, to save themselves, they had to abandon the raft and swim back to the ship. It was the third mate, Visser, watching anxiously from the *ODYSSEUS*, who realised that one of them, a French fireman who could not swim well, was in trouble. Without hesitation he plunged into the water, swam over to the raft and brought the man back alongside.

On the mole the mate Lindeman, realising that the sea wall would offer little protection against the flames now closing in, quickly got his party back into the boat, also collecting some refugees from other ships who preferred to take the chance of survival aboard the *ODYSSEUS*. It must have seemed a rash decision to those seeing her battered hull close up for the first time.

The main problem impeding her escape was that of motive power. Though chief engineer Jongsma was able to report that the steam pipes down below were intact and the engines still in working order, without her funnel the loss of draught was defeating every effort in the stokehold to goad life into her sullen furnace fires.

Frustratingly and frighteningly, whilst the *ODYSSEUS* remained a virtually dead ship all the heat, and more, needed to check her falling pressure gauge was being generated all round, glowing from still flaming wrecks and burning dangerously close to her over the waters of the harbour. The situation on deck was dismal indeed with no hopes of getting enough steam through to the windlass to raise her anchors.

In so precarious a situation precipitate measures were called for yet it was ingenuity that prevailed. Between them the deck and engineroom departments found the solution.

Someone thought of the hatchboards. They were the only objects in the ship of suitable length for use in the construction of a tall enough duct to replace in part the height of the missing funnel. It was the only hope left to get the air flowing once more through the stokehold.

Already the engineroom crew had hammered into some sort of shape the twisted and buckled steel which was all that remained of the original smoke stack. Using it as a base willing hands urgently and ingeniously raised above the gaping hole a multi-sided shaft, praying it would not catch fire whilst fervently hoping for the uplift of air.

Braced inside with salvaged and commandeered metal bars, wedged and lashed around with chain and stayed with wire, its ludicrous appearance belied its immediate importance. Encouraging cries from below proclaimed that the fires were drawing again, not vigorously but heartily enough to add to the low head of steam on which all hopes of survival depended.

Above, it was clear the time had arrived to move on. The approaching flames were uncomfortably near. The hot smuts from the burning oil were falling on the decks and added to the acrid stench of the night was the smell of blistering paint. Jacob Ouwehand, perspiring freely, his straw locks more spiky than ever was on the poop with the second mate and another sailor waiting for the order to hack through the stern moorings.

The heat had become almost unbearable by the time the word was given. Using fire axes and hacksaws they severed the remaining wires and dashed for safety. On the fo'c'slehead the shackle pins on both cables were knocked out and the anchors slipped. The *ODYSSEUS* was vibrating again to the beat of her engines and the steady turn of her screw.

Aftermath in the port of Bari. Ships still blaze among the wreckage.
A Bofers gun crew is closed up, but for once the Luftwaffe
had no need to return.
(Courtesy of Imperial War Museum A12745)

Painfully slowly through the narrowing channel between the leaping flames and the inhospitable wall she crept to the entrance and limped safely out into the Adriatic. If the enemy returned, as well they might, she would face them alone. Looking towards Bari as she dawdled waiting for the dawn, her crew thought it unlikely. Viewing the flames and smoke from beyond the moles it seemed the destruction was complete. In the daylight, under the pall of smoke through which hungry flames still flared, the chaotic scene of utter devastation sombrely confirmed the extent of the Luftwaffe's triumph. Bari, the only major supply port on Italy's east coast was out of action and would remain so for some time to come.

Jack Ridler, dumping overboard some of the shattered furniture from his cabin on the boatdeck, caught the disapproving eye of Captain Ruig. It was a subconscious reflection, a reminder perhaps that company property would still need to be accounted for. Against the vast destruction of the night it came as a first sign of returning reality.

Altogether, it transpired, seventeen merchant ships had been totally destroyed or sunk, eight others had been badly damaged and more than 1,000 seamen, service personnel and some civilians had died with others in hospital still to succumb from the effects of the Allies' own mustard gas. Some 40,000 tons of vitally needed war supplies had been blown up or burnt and the port facilities wrecked. It was a major set back to Allied plans.

For the *ODYSSEUS* the immediate need was to get her wounded to hospital and to land the crew members of other ships who had found refuge aboard. In response to her signals a motor torpedo boat arrived alongside to take them, including Captain Ruig, ashore. There was astonishment at her battered condition and the strange substitution for her funnel.

A weary senior officer of the naval control staff examined her dubiously. He questioned her chances of making her way to another port unaided, but bowed to her crew's declaration of faith. Battered as she was, to them the *ODYSSEUS* had nothing more to prove when it came to survival and all aboard, especially those who had sailed in her for over a year, had few doubts about her safe arrival.

With her remarkable funnel providing the gentle air stream to keep her vital spark alive, under the temporary command of her mate, she made her slow way to Brindisi, sixty miles to the south, to lick her wounds and await the return of her Captain. Such extensive damage would take time to repair and for her the Mediterranean campaign was over, but Holland would see her again and, in the less violent times to come, so would the Middellandsche Zee.

L'ENVOI

The *ODYSSEUS* survived the war to sail again from Amsterdam on frequent voyages to those same bright seas which had so recently held as much peril as the azure sky they again innocently reflected. Restored to her peacetime smartness, her prow and rails picked out in white to match the spotless paintwork above her gleaming black hull, she looked her old trim self again except in one respect.

Her new funnel was a less impressive substitute for that well proportioned masterpiece her Hamburg builders had provided more than twenty years before. Even the two broad white bands round the black stack, her company's symbol, could not disguise the fact that no-one had deemed it commercially worthwhile to replace it with something more becoming. If it was through any belief that her useful service was drawing to its close she would, for nearly two more decades, confound that presumptuous slight.

The bond which drew together those who had sailed in her from Britain in that critical period of the war also proved too strong to disappear quickly. Though seamen lose touch very often once their havens have been achieved it was not to be so with those of the *ODYSSEUS*.

With those old log books so recently disinterred, I found letters from many of those British and Dutch shipmates written over the next three or four years. It was cheerful correspondence in the main, not dwelling on the hard times, yet clearly acknowledging that lingering interdependence that had been thrust upon us.

Towards the end of the war I was to meet from time to time several members of the Dutch crew at favoured London haunts and found the bond of fellowship undiminished. I saw Eric Adams again. He was serving in a much larger cargo ship just back from the West Indies and a later letter informed me he had got a berth sailing from the Thames. I hoped to see him again for he was a good friend, but somehow I never did.

Apart from Jack Ridler with whom I never lost touch, the last of the crew I ever saw was Jim van Ommeren. Jack and I were together at the time. He was then radio officer in a tanker and our courses having converged we adjourned to "The Prospect of Whitby", then still a traditional watering hole for seamen, dockworkers and lightermen in The Pool of London.

ODYSSEUS (1,100 grt) - restored to her peacetime colours, with a new funnel and her scars concealed, sails again on her peaceful occasions. Built at Hamburg in 1922 she served the K.N.S.M. for almost 30 years and continued in the service of other owners for another decade before foundering in the Caribbean Sea in 1963.

(Courtesy of Nedlloyd)

Berthed nearby was an impressive Rotterdam registered cargo ship. It seemed too much to hope for, but neither of us was surprised to find Jim standing at the bar earnestly engaged in nautical chat. He was wearing his faded dungaree jacket and trousers and wore a familiar tweed cap which he swore was the one we had known for so long.

It was a joyful reunion in which much more was exchanged. He was clearly in his element once more and at his amusing best. I was never to see him or hear of him afterwards, though I made several attempts to trace him after Holland had been liberated. I can only hope he eventually came to anchor in some interesting haven to suit his whimsical and generous nature. I think it would have to be Rotterdam.

The last communication I had from any of the Dutch crew was in a letter from Gibraltar well after the war. It was from Jaapy Ouwehand, then serving in the *ORPHEUS*, another survivor of the K.N.S.M. fleet which had never been far from us in the Mediterranean. At that time she was outward bound from Amsterdam to Malta in her old pre-war trade, calling at several ports on the way in a five weeks round trip which he made sound idyllic.

It gave me news of the Bo'sun then serving in another of the company's ships, yet never mentioned something I was to discover later - that Jaapy and four members of the relief crew had been awarded the Dutch Cross of the Order of Merit following an official British report on the crew's conduct during the debacle at Bari. Captain Ruig, I learned, had been awarded the M.B.E. Of his future I heard nothing and to me at least he will remain an enigma.

Jack Ridler was to graduate from the London School of Economics soon after the war, about the time I returned to journalism. After many years on the staff of the American Embassy in Paris he is back in his native Gloucestershire, in a venerable house overlooking his beloved Severn.

This book owes much to him for he it was who inspired the re-reading of the evocative notes I scribbled so long ago. He also played an important role in rekindling my memory on incidents that somehow escaped my pen, though in no way can he be held responsible for any shortcomings in their ultimate presentation.

Whenever we met or corresponded, as we did frequently over the years, it was inevitable that we should often think of the *ODYSSEUS* and her crew. Yet neither of us did more than ponder over her ultimate fate. She remained with the K.N.S.M. fleet for nearly a decade after those perilous events. Occasionally I noted her movements, but eventually lost track of her altogether.

I had sadly concluded that, in the inevitable way in which most ships end up as so much scrap metal, she had gone to the breakers. Then to my joy I heard that she was still afloat under another name. In that brisk shipping market of the post-war era she was to change ownership four times in all, acquiring different names so rapidly it was not long before she had steamed beyond trace again.

In 1952 she became the *AIAS* and three years later the *AEOLOS* under the Greek flag. In 1957, for a longer spell, she was the *MARIA TERESA*. Then in 1961, when she was approaching her fortieth year of almost unbroken voyaging, she was sold for the last time to be renamed the *MADRID*, registered in Panama.

Although she had continued to sail in familiar Mediterranean waters for much of her extended career she was to end her days trading between the Caribbean ports she had known in her earlier years under the Dutch flag.

After loading at Puerto Cortes in Honduras towards the end of April 1963, she sailed for San Juan in Puerto Rica with a cargo of lumber on what proved to be her last voyage. It was towards the end of that 1,500 miles passage that the mounting years caught up with her. She foundered off Alta Vela in the Dominican Republic and her long enduring, war-scarred hull now lies fathoms deep in the historic waters of Hispaniola.

If ever a ship belied a name so boldly endowed with the savour of martial adventure it was the unpretentious cargo steamer *ODYSSEUS*. To me, on first sight, even her grey war paint seemed an irony. Yet when her real test came, she quickly and repeatedly proved her outright title to it. I can think of no better resting place for her old wrought iron plates than in those time-honoured waters of propitious discovery.

Index of Ships and Locations